External Timber Furniture

Timber Design File 11

EDGAR STUBBERSFIELD

Copyright © 2018 Rachel Stubbersfield

All rights reserved.

ISBN: 0-9944157-3-7
ISBN-13: 978-0-9944157-3-8

Contents

Introduction 1

1 Functional Aspects 2

Designing for Universal Access 3

Table heights from AS1428 4

Seats 5

Suggested dimensions for park settings 7

Location 8

The limitations of AS1428.2 8

Disabled access 9

2 Timber Species Selection 11

Introduction 11

Selecting the right species 12

Selecting the right grade 16

Specification for pine 17

Specification for cypress 18

Specification for Australian hardwood 18

Robust furniture 19

Heart in hardwood for robust furniture 19

Refined architectural pieces 20

Recycled Hardwood 20

Kiln Drying 20

Preservation 21

Over Ordering 23

Reasonable Expectations 23

3 Solid Timber 24

Normal Sizes 24

- Larger, non-standard sizes 26
- Surface Finish 27
- What sizes to use 28

4 Glued Timber 30

5 Round Timber 32

- Machined rounds up to 42 mm diameter 32
- Machined rounds over 42 mm diameter. 32
- Natural rounds 35
- Machined pine rounds 36

6 Detailing Frames and Fasteners 37

- Painting Steel Supports 41
  - Decorative finishes 42
  - Corrosion Resistant Finishes 42

7 Detailing Timber Components 43

- Drawings 43
- Fastening horizontal members 43
- Housed joints 45
- Slope of grain 47
- Corners 48
- Contacting the ground 49
- Overhang and distance between supports 50
- Detailing furniture containing large section timbers 51
- Detailing large section freestanding pieces 52

8 Leaching and Finishes 55

- Robust public furniture 55
  - Hardwood 55
  - Pine 56
  - Refined Architectural Pieces 56

 Leaching of Tannins 57

 Film Finishes 58

 Paint 59

 Clear Film finishes 61

 Penetrating Oils 63

 Lanolin Based Oils 65

 Painting Steel Frames 66

9 Applying Finishes and Maintenance 67

 Oil Based Finishes 67

  Consideration with new or recycled timber 67

  Maintenance when penetrating oil finish is in good condition 67

  Maintenance with oil when film finish has started to deteriorate 68

10 Thinking Away From the Standards 70

11 Design Checklist 74

Source of Images 78

Bibliography 79

About the Author 81

ACKNOWLEDGMENTS

I would like to acknowledge the invaluable assistance given to me in critiquing the technical aspects of this book by Ralph Bailey of Guymer Bailey Architects and Peter Savage of Savage Consulting. The book has been further enhanced through a range of professionals permitting the use of copyright images for which I am grateful. Their copyright is acknowledged at the end of this book.

Introduction

This book provides information on designing external timber furniture using the three timber types available in Australia, pine, cypress and hardwood. I was prompted to write the guide after being called to inspect some very expensive, custom designed and fabricated furniture that had failed in service after a very short time. This furniture was very attractive when first built and very functional and, had it been kept indoors, would have given many years of excellent service. Unfortunately, this was not the case and it was exposed to a very harsh environment. The designer and the fabricator had little comprehension of the difference between the two environments and the toll it must take on timber. It became obvious that there was need for a guide to help professionals, especially those who are inexperienced with timber, produce well detailed drawings with appropriate specifications for trouble free furniture with wooden elements.

This book does not deal with creativity. Most who read this guide will be professional designers and I stand in awe of the extraordinary skill that some possess to be able to create. Continue to do what you do well but follow the information in this guide to produce detailing at best practice, for as our political masters keep reminding us, "The Devil is in the detail." Outstanding design and outstanding detailing will produce a result that sets your work on an entirely different level.

My experience in this field came from years of fabricating robust external hardwood furniture, mainly to clients' designs, for fully weather exposed applications such as in national parks. You could not describe these as refined architectural pieces, just functional and durable items. The more refined pieces need even closer attention to the design and the maintenance. As you read this book you will realise that there is no great mystery to making your designs a success. Get your timber species and grade correct and look after the details so your timber is free to move with the changes in the climate, don't trap moisture and then get the coating and maintenance right and it will succeed. Leave matters unresolved to the lowest price tenderer and you will have a very unhappy customer.

There are a few gaps where you will read "Image Not Available." Unfortunately, copyright restrictions meant I could not use some images that graphically illustrated points I was making. If you can help with alternate images I would be grateful. I welcome feedback on the contents of the book. No doubt it has shortcomings and these can be addressed in future editions.

Edgar (Ted) Stubbersfield.
August 2018

1 Functional Aspects

The design of timber furniture for public use starts with the consideration of the exposure risk which can vary significantly. You must ask:

- Is the furniture to be installed in full weather exposure – sun and rain with no cover
- Is it under a roof such as a shelter but still exposed to rain and sun from the sides, or
- Is it totally under a roof cover and will not be significantly affected by the sun and rain?

In a restaurant setting it is even conceivable that the same furniture could be used both inside the venue and also in an al fresco situation as well and so pieces from the same batch may be experiencing all three circumstances.

The location proposed affects important decisions relating to the type of furniture to be used, type of fixing and type of finish for the timber. Joint detailing is another important consideration relating to weather exposure. Today, with anti-discrimination regulations in force, as well as the normal functionality requirements for furniture design particularly for public places such as parks, cafes, picnic shelters, outdoor eating areas etc. the designer must take into account the different need for disabled persons, the aged and children. Functionality obviously involves design for the human body in all its ages, shapes and flexibility. There is much information available on ergonomics and anthropometrics so there is no excuse for furniture design being uncomfortable or difficult to use.

Figure 1.   The Eames lounge and Ottoman.

I live in hope that the royalties from this book will allow me to purchase a genuine Eames lounge and ottoman, a chair described as having "the warm, receptive look of a well-used first baseman's mitt." (In reality it probably won't finance an Aldi copy.) This iconic chair has been in constant manufacture without significant modification since 1956 because, with its moulded plywood, heavy leather padding, adjustable height and reclining action it allows the lounge to conform to almost any body. Its commercial success has seen it copied by a number of manufacturers.

This very comfortable chair highlights the problem with external furniture. Moulded plywood will disintegrate, the leather will not take the ravages of the sun and rain and overall it is far from being robust enough for commercial use. The designer must produce, not just code compliant (where applicable) but also comfortable furniture without any recourse to padding, height adjustment or reclining action. This is very challenging and a seeming impossibility.

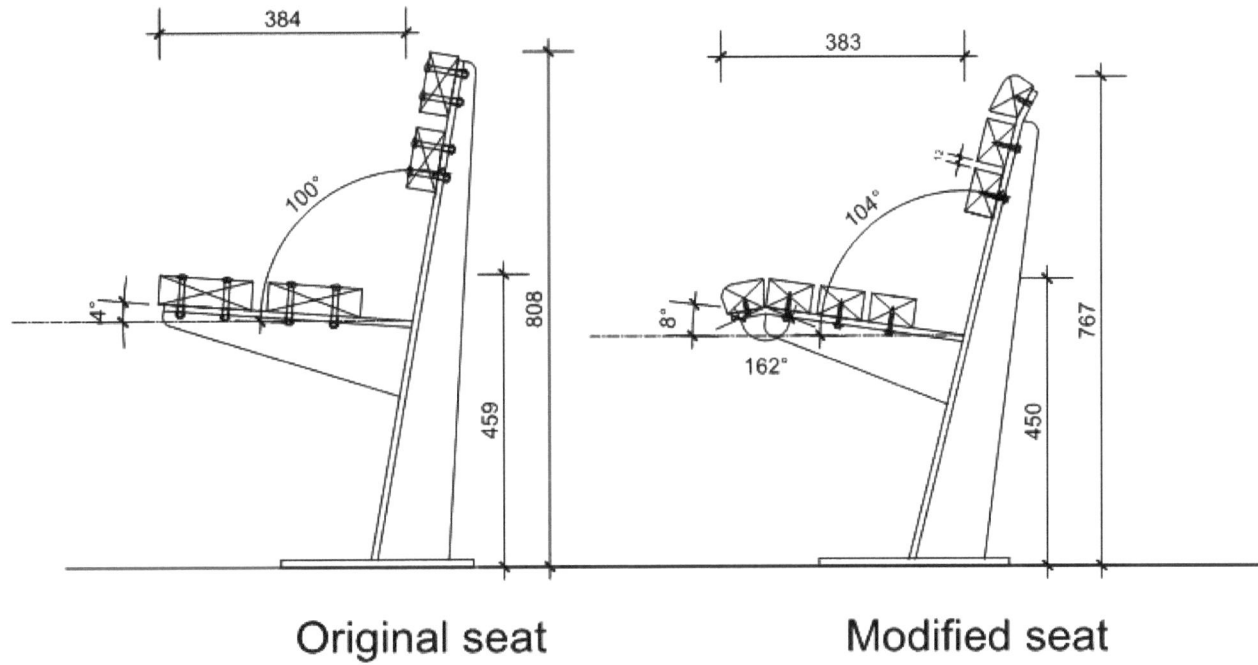

Figure 2. Slight differences between a comfortable and a very comfortable chair (in the authors opinion).

In the face of this design challenge, my advice would echo what Pablo Picasso is alleged to have said, "Good artists copy, great artists steal." One of the most important things that a furniture designer can do is, for lack of a better word, "steal". Let me explain. I used to make a comfortable steel framed seat with wooden slats (see 0) but, out one day with a friend, we sat on a competitor's seat and we had to agree that it was even more comfortable. The difference was primarily in the angle between the seat and the backrest and even then it was slight but I considered it worthwhile to change my design to replicate that improvement. This was not an exact copy of my competitor's design as both my competitor's seat and mine still looked very different and could not be confused. As you go about your daily affairs you will encounter a wide range of external furniture and it is very important to observe carefully and take note of what works and, just as importantly, what doesn't work and be prepared to learn, modify and improve.

Designing for Universal Access

You would expect for there to be a requirement for furniture used in public areas to *comply* with *AS1428.2 Design for access and mobility – Enhanced and additional requirements – Buildings and facilities*. Despite that I have observed that it often doesn't but, this is possibly more a deficiency of the standard rather than lack of care by designers. One reason for this is that the standard does not cover the full range of furniture that might be expected, such as free standing seats without backrests, furniture used when standing and low platforms. Notwithstanding, the Standard still gives practical guidance to assist designers but, ultimately, the range of disabilities that may be encountered means, and the

Standard acknowledges, that occasionally situations will arise where someone with a disability will find the facilities unsuitable.[1] As a consequence, the designer will need to consider carefully the needs of the actual users and this may involve designing away from the codes to achieve a specific outcome.

Note: This is not a full discussion of the requirements of AS1428.2 in regards to street furniture and the designer should read the full section and check if a later version of the standard referenced is available. Refer also to Chapter 10 where examples of furniture which lie outside of the Standard are illustrated.

Table heights from AS1428

Where a single table is being built the height can vary from 830 mm to 870 mm and the clearance under the can vary from 800 mm to 840 mm.[2] When two tables are provided the second unit's maximum height can vary from 730 mm to 770 mm with clearance from 710 mm to 750mm.[3] Against this, my own barbecue tables were built to 780 mm with clearance underneath of 735 mm which did not meet the code for either the first or second table. Non conformity with these dimensions is widespread, e.g. the main Queensland national parks table has at the time of writing, a height of 805 mm with a clearance under of 770.[4] The NSW tables had a height of 807 mm with a clearance underneath of 707 mm under the cross rail.[5] Again these are not complying tables.

Figure 3.   At 780 mm this proprietary table does not meet AS1428.2-1992

Further, these tables, in their disabled format, do not meet the required minimum clearance of 800 mm from the front of the table to an upright. I found similar non-conformance when measuring proprietary tables but not all while some manufacturers offered compliance to AS1428.2 as an option. My observations are:

- Non complying table heights and clearances are widespread, even the norm, and in particular are being widely used through national parks, on the east coast at least, without any issues.[6]
- The supply of a second table with the height at the lower end of 730 mm to 770 mm would prove too low for normal use and the practicality of this should be considered, particularly with barbecue tables, and
- There is merit in considering barbecue tables as a separate entity to a free standing table and a free standing seat.

---

[1] Standards Australia. AS1428.2 – 1992 *Design for access and mobility – Enhanced and additional requirements – Buildings and facilities.* (Homebush. Standards Australia: 1997) 24.1 NOTES.
[2] AS1428.2-1992 42.1.1
[3] AS1428.2-1992 42.1.2
[4] Queensland Government. *Queensland Parks and Wildlife Services Manual May 2003.* (No publication details) TAB1.1
[5] Outdoor Structures Australia *Drawing 050SD* which was copied from the original NSW design.
[6] I manufactured the Queensland design for 30 years without any feedback and the NSW design for about 10 years, again without any adverse feedback.

Seats

Seat heights are normally to be 450 mm high but AS1428.2 draws attention to the different height needs of different age groups. The height for older users should be up to 520 mm and for children and short people a height of 350 mm may be more appropriate. That is 180 mm difference! This flexibility is generally not available in proprietary products which invariably come with one height suits all users. The Standard advises that, if possible, a range of heights should be provided which can be done when designing custom furniture for a project. This should present little problem for locally made proprietary seating when they are made from fabricated steel or aluminium but impossible with cast frames. Where seats of varying heights are used, signage indicating intended users would be prudent. It should be noted that a child seat at 350 mm coupled with the recommended height of the table of up to 870 mm would be very impractical.

Figure 4. Many seat frames can be readily modified to suit different height requirements.

Figure 5. A custom fabricated seat incorporating a range of seat heights

The recommended width of the seat is between 400 to 450 mm[7] but this would need to be given thought if lower seats were being planned for children and short people. In these instances this depth of seat would be very uncomfortable and cut into the back of the knees. Note also that perfectly adequate barbecue tables, without backrests, may have seats that are only 250 mm wide and seldom wider than 300 mm.

All freestanding[8] seats are to be provided with armrests situated within the centre of gravity and at a height of 260 mm +- 40 mm above the seat. These are generally not provided on barbecue table seats presumably as the table can be used to assist people with disabilities in rising. Because stroke victims generally lose mobility on one side, the seat either has to have a rest at both ends or a single rest, centrally located to accommodate this. Despite the Standards requirements for armrests on all freestanding seats, at the time of writing it is very common for the seats to be supplied without them. In a large public facility you would expect at least a third of the seats to have arm rests. All edges and

---

[7] AS1428.2-1992, Figure 22.
[8] The illustrations in AS1428.2, Figure 22 are for free standing seats.

projection that can come in contact with the public should have a minimum radius of 5 mm[9] except for the front of the seat which should be at least 30 mm.[10]

The seat are required to have 20 mm fall from front to back and the angle between the seat and the backrest cannot exceed a maximum of 105 degrees. The depth of the seat should not exceed 100 mm and the user should be able to adjust their feet up to 150 mm under the seat to assist with rising by getting leverage close to the centre of gravity. The total height of the backrest is to be between 750 to 790 mm.[11]

Suggested dimensions for park settings

Ralph Bailey, a very experienced architect and furniture designer, considers that two distinct dimension sets are needed for park settings; one for wheelchair access and the other for when wheelchairs do not need access. His experience has led him to adopt the following dimensions as appropriate for the different applications:

	Top of Table	Clearance under	Seat Height	Longitudinal gap between table and seat
Range	830-870 mm	800-840 mm	500	70-100 mm
Usually	850 mm	815 mm		

Table 1. Recommended dimensions for wheelchair access park setting

He believes that 500 mm should be adopted for the seat height instead of 450 mm as the seat is simply too low for children when the table is at 850 – 870 mm. As well, this higher dimension is closer towards the 520 mm recommended for older users and is an acknowledgement of the simple fact that our community is ageing.

	Top of Table	Clearance under	Seat Height	Space between table and seat
Usual	730 mm	Not so critical	430	70-100 mm

Table 2. Recommended dimensions for non-wheelchair access park setting

A review of information from manufacturers of proprietary tables shows similar dimensions are widely adopted.

---

[9] AS1428.2-1992 27.1 (d)
[10] AS1428.2-1992 27.1 (c)
[11] AS1428.2-1992, Figure 32.

Location

Street furniture must be situated a minimum of 500 mm from path[12] and, ideally, on one side of the path only. An important consideration when designing furniture is that they are to have a colour contrast to the background of at least 0.3 (30%)[13] Green painted furniture against a grass background would be unsuitable.

The limitations of AS1428.2

Figure 6. Sitting and lounging are both possible on this unit.

While standards are useful servants they can be bad masters through limiting a designer's questioning of the full extent of what needs to be provided in a given location. The major limitation of designing to only meet AS1428.2 is that it assumes that all people want to do in a public space is sit with a straight back. The professional designer will find in coming years that the increasing popularity of outdoor spaces is going to see a demand for increasingly sophisticated requirements in what is provided. Areas to lounge, facilities to wash hands and charge phones are all considerations which are outside of the Standard but will become increasingly important.[14]

---

[12] AS1428.2-1992 27.1 (a)

[13] AS1428.2-1992 27.1 (b)

[14] Tietz, Christian. *People-friendly furniture in public places matters more than ever in today's city* URL: https://theconversation.com/people-friendly-furniture-in-public-places-matters-more-than-ever-in-todays-city-83568 Date Accessed: June 8, 2018.

Disabled access

Figure 7. Good disabled access, poor general access.

Figure 8. Better general access.

The table shown in Figure 7 has good wheelchair inclusion but still fails best practice in design because of the use of cross bars to support the seat. Cross bar type construction is very common as it is simple and inexpensive and is almost universal in the robust timber tables seen in national parks. This is understandable due to the constraints of having to supply large numbers of low maintenance tables at relatively low price at locations where people would be generally more mobile. But disability is more than just being restricted to wheelchairs and includes the general lack of flexibility of an aging population. While I thought nothing of supplying the table in Figure 7 thirty years before writing this book, now that the years have taken their toll, I realise how undesirable anything is that hampers access. The same table is shown in Figure 8 but the seats are free standing which is far more preferable.

Figure 9. A standard National Parks barbecue table extended to allow disabled access

Figure 10. This table is more inclusive for disabled users. (Design is copyright Guymer Bailey Architects)

The two tables shown in Figure 9 and Figure 10, both supplied by the author, show how two different designers have approached the requirements of disabled access. The one "parks" the wheelchair bound user out at the end, almost as an afterthought and away from the "action" whereas the other started with the need of the disabled user first and the triangular design incorporates up to three chairs fully into the group. This inclusion is all done with superior aesthetics.

2 Timber Species Selection

Introduction

Satisfactory performance in structural applications such as roof trusses give no indication of suitability for external furniture. In that application there is no weather exposure or a critical eye. By contrast, external furniture must endure the most demanding applications that timber can be exposed to and still retain good aesthetics. This requires great care in the specification because all timbers were not created equal especially when it comes to weather exposed applications. Side by side with correct specification consideration should also be given to confirmation of grade compliance. Factors influencing the timber choice are:

- Horizontal members compound the effect of heat, cold, wind and rain with the top face being far more stressed than the underside or those that are vertical
- Far less weathering is acceptable than would be tolerated on other weather exposed applications such as in bridges and cross arms on a power pole, and
- The effects of the weather can be minimised by suitable maintenance but most furniture will experience either inadequate or no maintenance at all.

Success is dependent on four factors, each equally important. These are:

- Selecting the correct species
- Selecting the correct size
- Selecting and receiving the correct grade
- Getting the design details correct, and
- Correct maintenance.

This chapter will assist you in understanding the importance of the selecting the correct species and give guidance in how to specify an appropriate grade. The following chapter will drill deeper and give further guidance in determining what sizes should be used.

Figure 11. This pine barbecue setting in the UK is performing without any problems.

Figure 12. This remnant from a pine setting from Queensland shows the effect of a harsh climate.

Selecting the right species

Just as timbers are not created equal, neither are all climates. The environment the timber is subjected to has a big impact on the type of timber which will perform satisfactorily. For most of Australia, unpainted softwoods used in horizontal applications and exposed to the full effects of the weather will give very poor performance as the climate is just too harsh. Constant wetting and drying of the horizontal surfaces will see them "self-destruct." Take that same pine item to the UK and, without the same heat and UV, there will be much slower degrade of the horizontal surfaces. Micro reeded finish, also called a rougher headed finish, is a worthwhile initiative on pine as, apart from some appearance benefits, it also seems to hold coating systems better because the increased surface area and the ridges ensure a good thickness of paint. Ultimately, it will not save the piece from the impact of significant moisture cycling and the propagation of splits, particularly on horizontal surfaces.

Subject to the limitations caused by fastener damage, when pine is used in vertical members it should perform satisfactorily as it does not experience the same degree of moisture cycling. I would not recommend pine unless it is used in conjunction with very high quality, vapour impermeable coating, as any minor checking will propagate over time and significantly affect appearance and can promote decay. For most of mainland Australia hardwood will be the obvious solution for the horizontal members.

In Australia we have two other options, white cypress, more commonly known as cypress, and as mentioned, hardwood which can either be local or imported. Cypress is a softwood whose colour ranges from light yellow through orange to light brown. The heartwood of Cypress is very durable, almost an In Ground 1 and has superb natural termite resistance. The difficulty is with the white coloured sapwood which, like all sapwood, is Durability Class 4, but, unlike the sapwood of hardwood and pine, is very resistant[15] to commercially available waterborne treatments[16]. Because of the small log size and

---

[15] Department of Agriculture and Fisheries. *White Cypress*. URL: https://www.daf.qld.gov.au/forestry/using-wood-and-its-benefits/wood-properties-of-timber-trees/white-cypress. Date Accessed: 3 October 2017.

[16] I am aware that kiln dried 19 mm cypress was successfully treated with light organic solvent preservative. This treatment is known as LOSP. Theoretically it is possible to treat any kiln dried cypress with LOSP.

larger section size that may be required, significant portions of any cypress order will contain sapwood. This means that any untreated item containing sapwood will be satisfactory under a patio roof as, unlike some hardwoods, it is not attacked by insects. A different outcome will result if it is moved outside. Because of this, I would not recommend cypress for external furniture unless it can be purchased free of sapwood. This is possible with members such as 100x100 mm which can be supplied as a box heart member (The heart of white cypress is stable unlike hardwood) but the difficulty is with say 150x50 mm for the seats and tops. A further factor working against cypress was put succinctly by a cypress miller with many years' experience, "The sun will dry the cypress out excessively and it will crack and look terrible."[17]

Figure 13. Kwila/Merbau used for seat slats

Kwila/Merbau has a long history of use in external furniture and its performance has been adequate though extra attention has to be given to the issue of leaching as this species has a very high level of extractives. In the same way, teak has a good reputation used in similar situations. A wide range of hardwoods is now being offered with impressive durability claims but these should not be accepted blindly. Other hardwoods should only be used with great care and research[18]. Numerically similar durability classes from Europe and other countries can reflect a much shorter life expectancy than in Australia. Examination of the information in Table 3 shows that durable timbers (class 1 and class 2) are expected to perform a lot longer in Australia than in many other countries. Even when the service life is similar, variable factors including climate, UV, pathogens, testing methodology and intellectual rigour[19] mean there is still no correlation to Australian values. This makes it unsound to compare Australian durability ratings with those used by other countries. A good example is the use of Robinia in playgrounds. This species would have a rating of 1 in Europe but under Australian conditions is likely to be an In Ground 3. Always ask for Australian ratings and for aged examples of an unfamiliar species that can be inspected. The matter is fraught with too many problems to move away from a timber with longstanding history of successful use to be a "guinea pig" for a new species.

---

[17] Wildman, Errol. *Pers. Com.* 4 October 2017.
[18] The first place I would look is *Construction Timbers in Queensland* and followed by Bootle's *Wood in Australia*.
[19] In this category may fit the early description of Garo Garo as a durable timber based on Papua New Guinea data and later downgraded after many failures in Australia.

Class	1	2	3	4	5
	\multicolumn{5}{c}{Probable life in years[20]}				
Aust above-ground[21]	> 40	15 to 40	7 to 15	0 to 7	
Aust in-ground[22]	> 25	15 to 25	5 to 15	0 to 5	
UK[23]	>25	15-25	10-15	5-10	<5
EU[24]	?	?	?	?	?
China[25]	> 9	6 to 8	2 to 5	< 2	
Japan[26]	> 9	7 to 8.5	5 to 6.5	3 to 4.5	< 2.5
Malaysia[27]	> 10	5 to 10	2 to 5	< 2	
Bangladesh[28]	> 3	2 to 3	1 to 2	< 1	
Tanzania[29]	> 10	5 to 10	2 to 5	1 to 2	< 1
Brazil[30]	> 8	5 to 8	2 to 5	< 2	
USA[31]	?	?	?	?	
Canada	?	?	?	?	

Table 3. Different international durability scales.

---

[20] A considerable degree of caution should be exercised with these expected life expectancies, particularly for unpainted horizontal surfaces.
[21] Standards. AS 5604-2005 …, Table 1.
[22] Standards. AS 5604-2005 …, Table 1.
[23] The durability classes in BS EN 350-1 are now termed DC1 to DC5. The service lives are from the Building Research Establishment's *A Handbook of Softwoods* last edition published in 1977, now out of print. Sycamore, Janet. Pers Com. 25 April 2018. There aren't separate classifications for in and above ground applications
[24] Despite the same standard being used in Europe as in the UK, the same expectancy does not apply. At the time of writing there is no uniform "European approach to link durability classes to service lives or service life categories" nor is there agreement on these categories. Brischke, Christian. *Pers. Com.* 12 June 2021. Contact the writer for further information.
[25] Stirling, Rod. *Natural Durability Classification Systems Used Around the World*. Paper presented at The International Research Group on Wood Protection conference, Beijing, China May 2009. Reference: IRG/WP 09-10694, 5.
[26] Stirling. *Natural* …, 6.
[27] Stirling. *Natural* …, 6.
[28] Stirling. *Natural* …, 6.
[29] Stirling. *Natural* …, 6.
[30] Stirling. *Natural* …, 6.
[31] Timber durability standards in the USA and Canada are less evolved than in Australia and Europe and there no standards for natural durability similar to AS 5604. Stirling. Natural …, 4-5.

While best success should come from Australian hardwoods, it is inadequate just to specify "Australian hardwood" or something like "F14 hardwood." Only the most durable of the over 200 species that are milled commercially will suffice.[32] Those that are the most durable include the ironbarks, tallowwood, spotted gum, grey gum and Gympie messmate. Because of their high strength and durability they were known under the very useful trade term as the "royal species".

Two of these royal species are of particular interest for external furniture, spotted gum and tallowwood because they contain natural oils which make them greasy to touch.[33] These oils assist in providing superior weathering. This is in stark contrast to a timber like blackbutt (Figure 14) which is dry to the touch and weathers far less graciously. This greasiness can make gluing difficult and, particularly with tallowwood, can cause difficulties with timber finishes.

Figure 14.   Degradation of 13 year old blackbutt table tops in SE Queensland.

The availability of spotted gum is extremely good as it comprises a little under 70%[34] of the timber harvested from timber state forests in Queensland. It also has the advantage of containing the least amount of extractives of any of the Australian hardwoods. Tallowwood is much less common making up about 1.25% of the New South Wales forestry harvest and even less common in Queensland. Notwithstanding, the smaller amounts of timber required for most outdoor furniture mean that tallowwood can be a viable option despite it being less common. Others species that were reported to the author as having proved successful for external furniture are the less readily available Queensland species, satinay (though it must be seasoned due to high shrinkage) and white beech (very low shrinkage) and, as mentioned earlier, teak.[35]

In the southern states, Victorian ash/Tasmanian oak are commonly available species but their low

---

[32] I found one manufacturer that claimed In Ground Durability 3 was adequate for weather exposed applications such as furniture. URL: http://www.bottonandgardiner.com.au/about-us/environmental-policy Date Accessed: October 4, 2017.

[33] Department of Agriculture and Fisheries. *Spotted Gum*. URL: https://www.daf.qld.gov.au/forestry/using-wood-and-its-benefits/wood-properties-of-timber-trees/spotted-gum. Date Accessed: 3 October 2017. Department of Agriculture and Fisheries. *Tallowwood*. URL: https://www.daf.qld.gov.au/forestry/using-wood-and-its-benefits/wood-properties-of-timber-trees/tallowwood. Date Accessed: 3 October 2017.

[34] Based on figures 2003 to 2013 from state forests and grazing leases and not expected to change in the short term. Seibuhr, Jane. *Pers. Com.* 12 Feb, 2015.

[35] Bailey, Ralph. *Pers. Com.* 14 November 2017.

durability[36] preclude their use in external furniture though it has been known to give satisfactory service as patio furniture. In Western Australia, different species predominate, mainly jarrah and karri. Despite an abundance of claims that the timber is highly durable[37] both are Above Ground Durability 2 timbers.[38] Jarrah would be preferred over karri as it has higher in ground durability suggesting better overall performance and also karri "does not have a good reputation for paint holding"[39] so there may be problems if a film finish is used. The question is whether jarrah should be used as, in the eastern states, an In Ground Durability 2 timber would be considered unsuitable?

Jarrah has been used in patio furniture for a long time and is readily available at any number of stores and at premium prices as befits its beauty. On surveying manufacturers in WA they had no doubt about its suitability with claims of very long life expectancy though not all timber resellers agreed.[40] But it simply does not have the durability that is expected and there are far more appropriate red timbers available from the East Coast.[41] My own experience is through exporting spotted gum decking to Japan. Invariably, their love for the colour red meant that many projects went to jarrah. There were a number of high profile failures and the market which did not have the subtlety to differentiate between different Australian species was all but lost.

Selecting the right grade

A highly durable timber will not achieve the desired result if the grade is not high also. There are four structural grades recognised under AS 2082 Timber - Hardwood - Visually stress-graded for structural purposes and . These are:

- Structural Grade 1 representing timber with 75% of the strength of clear timber
- Structural Grade 2 representing timber with 60% of the strength of clear timber
- Structural Grade 3 representing timber with 48% of the strength of clear timber
- Structural Grade 4 representing timber with 38% of the strength of clear timber

---

[36] The four species that make up the Victorian ash/Tasmanian oak group are Above Ground Durability 3. Department of Agriculture and Fisheries. *Tasmanian Oak*. URL: https://www.daf.qld.gov.au/forestry/using-wood-and-its-benefits/wood-properties-of-timber-trees/tasmanian-oak. Date Accessed: 3 October 2017.

[37] E.g., Auswest Timbers claims "Karri is an extremely durable hardwood, renowned for its strength and beauty" *Karri Hardwood Furniture*. URL: http://auswesttimbers.com.au/product/karri-hardwood-furniture/ Date accessed: 7 October 2017.

[38] Department of Agriculture and Fisheries. *Jarrah*. URL: https://www.daf.qld.gov.au/forestry/using-wood-and-its-benefits/wood-properties-of-timber-trees/jarrah. Date Accessed: 3 October 2017. Bootle, Keith R. *Wood in Australia, Types Properties and Uses, Second Edition*. (McGraw Hill: Sydney, 1983) 291.

[39] Bootle, Keith R. *Wood in Australia, Types Properties and Uses, Second Edition*. (McGraw Hill: Sydney, 1983) 291.

[40] One furniture manufacturer, with practical experience since 1982 said, "Put a piece of Jarrah outside, all that happens if untreated it goes gray (like all timber) but it will stay structurally perfect for decades." Flynn, Bill. *Pers. Com.* October 6, 2017. One dissenting voice said "Unfortunately due to successful lobbying by our friends in the Greens and Labour governments all the good Jarrah has been locked up and mills are being forced to mill juvenile and lower grade material to supply markets, as with any specie, mature wood preforms far better." Law, Brett. *Pers. Com.* October 10, 2017.

[41] The comments of an east coast manufacturer explains it well and is in keeping with the previous footnote: "We used to use it for all of our furniture until about 10/15 years ago as pricing increased. Quality and durability was excellent. We used Kwilla/Merbau for the majority of our work since then until about 2 years ago, as our customers pushed for a more sustainable option. We now use spotted gum as a preference as the quality/weathering is reasonable, pricing is good and all of our customers are happy with the choice. We have used Jarrah on a few jobs in the last couple of years where the customer has insisted. It is very expensive and the quality is terrible, I have been told this is due to the export market absorbing all of the quality materials. We avoid it like the plague now, as those couple of jobs suffered a large amount of re-work and scrap."

A similar arrangement to hardwood applies to pine in AS2856 Timber – Softwood – Visually stress graded for structural purposes where there are 5 structural grades. By matching the Strength Group i.e. structural properties of the species being graded to the amount of strength loss allowed under its Structural Grade, an F grade is achieved. For instance, unseasoned spotted gum (Strength Group 2) supplied in Structural Grade 2 (60% clear timber strength) achieves F17. Should that timber be supplied kiln dried it increases in strength and then F17 is achieved by timber which has defects so large that only 38% of its strength remains. Clearly, specifying, receiving and using timber of such low grade will result in a shorter service life, but probably more importantly, very poor aesthetics result long before the item is replaced. Both hardwood and pine has to be specified carefully to ensure that this does not happen.

Figure 15.   Large defect filled with "bog".

Specification for pine

The highly mechanised nature of pine sawmilling and processing will mean that you have less opportunity, if any, to purchase a custom grade for the timber that you use in outdoor settings. The specification for machine graded timber would be:

Horizontal members – MGP14 treated to H3 (not LOSP[42] or CCA), untreated sapwood not to exceed 20%
All other members – MGP 12 treated to H3(not LOSP or CCA), untreated sapwood not to exceed 20%

The timber should still be inspected and selected so the best face is presented to the weather. The fabricator should also be prepared to cull some material in line with the visual requirements below.

If the timber is to be visually graded the requirements are somewhere between clear grade and select grade as specified in AS 4785.2-2002[43] Timber - Softwood - Sawn and Milled Products Grade Description. This is summarised as:

---

[42] This is discussed under preservation further on in this chapter.
[43] Note that Part 3 of the standard deals with furniture components but Part 2 deals with decking which is closer in application to furniture sheltered from the weather.

Defect	Recommended[44]	Select grade	Clear grade
Tight knots	25% of surface	50% of surface[45]	Not permitted[46]
Checks and splits	Not permitted	not exceeding 1mm[47]	Not permitted[48]
End splits	Not permitted	Not permitted[49]	Not permitted
Sloping grain	Max 1:8	Max 1:5[50]	Max 1:5
Loose knots, holes, cone holes	Not permitted	Not exceeding 10 mm[51]	Not permitted
Resin streaks, resin pockets and bark pockets	Not permitted	Max. 6 mm wide x 50 mm long[52]	Not permitted[53]
Horizontal alignment	the heart or pith side of the boards should be placed in the downward side	Not mentioned	Not mentioned
Moisture content	Max 15%	Not mentioned in Part 2	Not mentioned in Part 2
Treatment	Sapwood treated to H3, heartwood not to exceed 20%	Not mentioned in Part 2	Not mentioned in Part 2

Table 4. Recommended grade compared to Clear and Select Grade

While clear grade timber is to be preferred, the grade proposed recognises the simple fact that it is probably not going to be readily available and some compromise on quality will have to be made. While this specification could be relaxed somewhat for the frame, a knot half the surface as permitted under an "appearance" grade is considered too high.

I would not consider pine as a suitable material for refined architectural pieces.

Specification for cypress

Should a designer decide to use cypress, a similar specification to that in Table 2 should be adopted.

Specification for Australian hardwood

It is envisaged that two types of hardwood furniture will be required, robust items and refined

---

[44] This recommendation is based on a document *The Effect of Timber Grade, Density, Size and Orientation on the mechanical Degradation of Timber Exposed to the Weather in Horizontal (Decking and Similar) Applications* – no publication details
[45] AS4785.2-2002 A4.2.2.1 (a).
[46] AS4785.2-2002 A4.3.1 (a)
[47] AS4785.2-2002 A4.3.1 (g).
[48] AS4785.2-2002 A4.2.2.1 (o) and (q).
[49] AS4785.2-2002 A4.2.1 (i).
[50] AS4785.2-2002 A1.3.
[51] AS4785.2-2002 A4.3.1 (b) (i).
[52] AS4785.2-2002 A4.3.1 (e)
[53] AS4785.2-2002 A4.2.2.1 (i), (j) and (k).

architectural pieces.

Robust furniture

For robust furniture, the grade descriptions of AS2082 are inappropriate for the horizontal members which need careful specification. If specifying to an F grade the physical appearance could be very poor. The timber will normally be "off the shelf" sizes free of heart but occasionally could be large sections such as 300x300 mm, 300x250 mm, 200x200 mm with heart in, their very size precluding any possibility of them being supplied heart free.

Heart free timber for robust furniture

The following specification will ensure the timber has appropriate aesthetics and minimal degradation from weathering.

Horizontal members – follow the Deckwood specification which requires freedom from the following on the sawn[54] (upper) face-

- Loose and unsound knots
- Shakes
- Loose Gum Veins
- Knot holes
- Termite Galleries
- Want, wane and bark
- Checks wider than 1 mm
- End splits wider than 1 mm
- Included bark
- Borer holes larger than 3 mm
- In addition,
    1. permitted defects shall not cover more that 15% of the top face.
    2. Permissible defects on the upper face may include 1 only borer hole up to 6mm diameter per plank.

Other members – graded to Structural Grade 2 – irrespective of species.

Heart in hardwood for robust furniture

My recommended specification for heart in timber for robust furniture is:

- Width in mm by thickness in mm, heart centre hardwood,
- Acceptable species are spotted gum, tallowwood and ironbark
- Cut with the heart in the centre, not significantly to one side.

---

[54] A sawn surface will weather far better than a dressed one. A very acceptable surface finish for commercial applications can be achieved by sanding .

- Cut an expansion joint/s into each face within one week of milling. The expansion joint/s will be 3 mm wide and 25 mm deep.
- Arris the edge of the expansion joint on the top face and
- Where timber is supplied with the heart significantly to one side acceptance is subject to the (insert profession)'s approval for use and give instructions as to placement

Refined architectural pieces

There is an appropriate Australian Standard, AS2796.3 Timber – Hardwood -Sawn and milled products Part 3: Timber for furniture components. There are three grades recognised under this standard, Select Grade, Medium Feature Grade and High Feature Grade and the grade that that should be specified is Select Grade. While the grade required for the vertical members does not need to be as high as the that for horizontal members, the grade description for medium feature is too low for external work. Natural features permitted under Medium Feature Grade includes loose gum veins, gum pockets, overgrowth of injury and knot checks. These can give character to internal furniture but are unsuitable for external furniture.

Timber processors are more used to working to AS2796.2 Hardwood -Sawn and milled products Part 2 Grade Description which applies to products such as decking. The differences in the Standards are slight and mainly relate to moisture content.

Recycled Hardwood

Recycled timber has become a "trendy" material to specify. (and good from a sustainable design point of view), but often there is little thought given to the consequences. It is thought that if the timber is cut from a piece of 100 year old timber it must be well seasoned but that is often nor the case. Timber cut from large sections will not be seasoned but behave exactly the same as freshly sawn timber. The large section sizes are simply too large to dry.

Taking tired, often worn out timber means that the timber cut from it will be the same. There are industry standards for recycled timber but they are very generous in the amount of defect allowed. As well timber cut from old powerpoles will likely contain CCA treatment which will not be permitted in furniture under APVMA guidelines.

By all means use recycled timber but do not drop the standard required.

Kiln Drying

Pine, for all intents and purposes is only available kiln dried and is used as it comes from the supplier. Hardwood has limited but increasing availability kiln dried. As it is not commercially possible to dry timber beyond 50 mm thick, this mean that items such as 100x100mm posts and 75 mm wide rails as would be found in robust furniture cannot be supplied kiln dried. With only the horizontal surfaces capable of being dried there seems to be little point in doing so for robust furniture providing that lower shrinkage timbers (up to 6%) are used and the design accommodates shrinkage.

For a refined architectural piece, the beauty of the timber is intended to be capitalised upon rather than just functional matters. In these situations the timber should be kiln dried. Unlike flooring where the moisture content is critical, there is considerable leeway with the moisture in timber used for external furniture when it is considered that it could be in the rain for a week. The requirement for light decking is between 18 and 10 percent[55] and for furniture is between 13 and 8 percent.[56] Weather exposed

---

[55] AS2796.1-1999, 4.2

furniture will have requirements more in keeping with light decking and I suggest a maximum of 15%.

Movement must be expected even with kiln dried timber given the wide range that can be experienced in the different parts of Australia as well as about a 3% change in the one locality over a year. A less well known measurement of shrinkage is "Unit Shrinkage" which is the dimension change for each percent change in moisture and for spotted gum that is 0.38%. This means that a 150 mm kiln dried piece still changes in dimension by 1.7 mm over the year. The designer should still design to accommodate shrinkage particularly when considering the gap between boards.

Preservation

Preservation is not an option despite some restrictions on which one is chosen. Any sapwood will decay in the weather and some sapwood contains starch which attracts lyctus attack which will turn that sapwood to powder even quicker. The table in Figure 17 shows untreated lyctus susceptible sapwood in tallowwood.

At the time of writing, there is no national quality assurance scheme for timber treatment and there can be serious issues with poorly treated pine. Given its low durability disappointing results can be experienced– see Figure 16. When treated with copper based preservatives (ACQ, Tanalith E), the timber supplied can be checked for treatment before use simply by looking at the end grain. Treated timber is markedly darker where it has penetrated.

One common and extremely effective preservative, CCA, is not permitted for use in external furniture under the requirements of the Australian Pesticides and Veterinary Medicines Authority (APVMA). The APVMA restrictions on CCA acknowledge that the risks are very low and do not require existing CCA treated furniture to be removed. In the section on coating, I provide guidance on how to effectively seal CCA.

Figure 16. Very badly decayed treated pine after 12 years.

---

[56] AS2796.3-1999 2.1

The two clear treatments are boron and LOSP. Boron is normally used for H1 (internal lyctus attack) applications and is approved for H2[57] (internal lyctus borers and termites) applications but is not used externally because it leaches. In reality, if constantly oiled with a water repellant or sealed with a film finish that is not allowed to break down, H2 would most likely suffice, but these conditions cannot be guaranteed and it will be difficult, as well, to find a company that treats to H2 with boron. LOSP is an effective preservative for kiln dried timber but treatment quality can vary considerably. Because of the high cost of the treatment chemical, some plants treat to "uptake" i.e. the process is stopped when the amount of chemical theoretically required has been used. Others treat to "retention" i.e. using sufficient chemical to achieve the minimum amount of chemical needed in all parts of the piece of timber. This can involve using more than 50% more chemical. To further complicate matters there are two different H3 treatments, one for vertical painted surfaces and another for horizontal unpainted surfaces and there is double the chemical needed for the horizontal application.[58] All in all, until a national quality assurance scheme for preservation is established, I believe it is best to avoid LOSP for fully weather exposed furniture situations. Alternatively, the designer may wish to undertake research about treatment plants in their locality.

IMAGE UNAVAILABLE

Figure 17. Untreated Lyctus susceptible sapwood.

The water based treatments available that are effective are Tanalith E and ACQ which will turn the sapwood of hardwood brown and that of pine, green. Normally, the sapwood will be more present on one side than the other so the face with the least sapwood should be presented during manufacture. Small amounts of timber can be supplied sapwood free, I readily acknowledge, but it requires a level of competence from sawmill workers and even tradesmen that sadly seems to be lacking. The table perimeter trim in Figure 17 had at least two inspections at the sawmill before it reached the joiner who also did not remove it. My advice, and this is based on hard learnt experience, is not to ask for timber free of sapwood.

CN Emulsion, an effective preservative which is frequently used in the joints of timber structures exposed to the weather, should not be used in furniture as the grease, which remains on the surface for a long time can stain clothes and transfer to hands etc. More useful would be to cut the components to length, drill all holes and then treat them with whatever preservative has been specified,

---

[57] AS1604.1, Table H2.
[58] AS1604.1, Table H2

Over Ordering

Figure 18. Natural feature in timber that should have been culled prior to manufacture.

As part of the timber specification there must be a requirement that, when the timber is ordered from the supplier, at least 5% extra than is required be ordered. The various Australian Standards that apply to timber anticipate that a 5% non-compliance is to be tolerated.[59] Further, rough sawn timber which is in grade may become out of grade after machining. At this stage natural features which are otherwise hidden could become exposed and gum veins will invariably become longer.

The edge piece shown in Figure 18 should not have been used and this can only happen if there is extra material to call upon.

Reasonable Expectations

Timber is not going to be like steel or aluminium or plastic, completely homogenous but without character. Because timber is a natural product some in service end splitting should be expected and is permitted under AS 2796.3-1999.[60]

---

[59] AS2796.3 – 1999, 3.1.4, AS2082 – 2007, 1.10.3.
[60] 3.1.5.

3 Solid Timber

While most external timber furniture is manufactured from "off the shelf" sizes, and this would certainly be the case with all refined pieces, there is also the need to consider larger, non-readily available sizes, particularly for robust furniture.

Normal Sizes

Hardwood is sawn in a range of standard sizes being 16, 25, 38, 50 and then in 25 mm increments up to 300 mm. Pine is generally sawn in a smaller range of sizes, with 125, 175 and 225 mm not being produced and the largest being 250 mm. These are not the sizes that you will be dealing with however. Sawing tolerances must be accommodated and further, kiln drying reduces timber in size and dressing even further reduces timber size. Pine is normally supplied as a dry processed product and the sizes normally available are

35mm thick, 70, 90, 140, 190 mm
45 mm thick, 70, 90, 140, 190, 240 mm

Pine can be further processed to produce a smaller size say 42x85 mm but larger sizes e.g. 50 mm thick is not possible.

Hardwood sizing is more complex as it can be supplied green off saw (GOS) rough sawn, GOS sized, GOS dressed all round (usually designated DAR), as well as kiln dried in the same options. All of these options are different sizes. The differences among these forms is explained below.

Rough Sawn Green Off Saw. This can best be understood as an approximate size only. AS2082 allows hardwood, on the day of milling, to be cut with a tolerance of + or − 3 mm. This means that 150x50 mm can be supplied anywhere between 147x47 to 153x53 mm. Remember, these measurements are on the day of milling only. Shrinkage then takes place as the timber seasons. This can vary between 6% (spotted gum) to 13% (turpentine). As was stressed in the chapter Timber Selection, specifications that just say F14 etc. are of no assistance as they do not refer to shrinkage, or other critical performance criteria including durability, stability or effectively deal with appearance.

Sized Green Off Saw. This is the same product as above except that it has passed through a planer and has been reduced to the minimum size allowed under the AS2082 i.e. 3 mm undersize. A tolerance of +/- 0.5 mm applies. Structural timber is frequently sized for height only but at the clients' request can be machined on a single face and edge. This does not produce "dressed timber" as a side and an edge are left rough sawn. For 150x50 mm sized one edge and one face, the timber is 147x47 mm. Timber for horizontal members in robust furniture will normally be sized for thickness and width whereas vertical members will probably be thicknessed for height, particularly if being used in jigs. Shrinkage still occurs.

Dressed Green Off Saw. The timber is dressed on all four sides termed dressed all round (usually designated DAR) and would not have pencil round edges unless specified (usually designated DPR). It is normally finished 5 mm under the nominal size. If you specify 150x50 dressed, the timber will normally be supplied as 145x45 mm. If you nominate 145x45 mm the producer will understand this to be the finished size. It is not generally feasible to have fractional sizes cut i.e. cut slightly oversise so you can finish 150x50 mm.

Dressed Seasoned. This is where the biggest problems come in as, very often, the dressed green off saw sizes are nominated and it is not possible to produce them simply. The way to calculate the finished size is as follows: deduct the sawing tolerance of 3 mm, then deduct the shrinkage for the species, (spotted gum is 6%) and then a further 2 mm for dressing. As an example, using 150 mm spotted gum, first deduct the 3 mm sawing tolerance leaving 147 mm, next deduct 6% shrinkage leaving 138 mm then finally allow 2mm for dressing giving 136 mm. The machining tolerance of 0.5 mm applies. The table below should be helpful.

	Sawing Tolerance	Green Sized	Green Dar	Dressed Seasoned
25	+/- 3 mm	22	20	19
38	+/- 3 mm	35	33	31
50	+/- 3 mm	47	45	42
75	+/- 3 mm	72	70	66
100	+/- 3 mm	97	95	90
125	+/- 3 mm	122	120	113
150	+/- 3 mm	147	145	136
175	+/- 3 mm	172	170	160
200	+/- 3 mm	197	195	183

Table 5. Standard sizes of Australian hardwoods with 6% shrinkage

This is further complicated as a limited number of millers are cutting oversize timber so as to produce a kiln dried size the same size as the green off saw dressed all round size e.g. 145x45.[61] But don't assume that the species you require is available in this slightly larger size. Check and obtain written confirmation of availability and lead time. The specification must nominate a supplier when the larger size is nominated. While there is a reluctance to mention suppliers by some specifiers this is vitally important when the material is not standard. It prevents the lowest priced tenderer "shopping around" to maximise his profit and leaving it too late to order. As delivery of any dry hardwood may take three months it can be prudent to request evidence of ordering.

As mentioned under *Kiln drying*, it introduces the need to consider "unit shrinkage", the percentage change in cross section for each percentage change in moisture content. It means that very small gaps may close up during the year.

---

[61] E.g. Parkside timbers. *Parkside Structural and Joinery Products* URL: http://parksidetimber.com.au/structural-joinery.html. Date accessed:9 October 2017

Larger, non-standard sizes

Figure 19.   Untreated pine heartwood has decayed leaving the treated sapwood.

The only real option for larger sizes is hardwood! Large pine sections involve the use of untreated (and untreatable) heartwood and heart (or pith). The piece of decking in Figure 19 shows that the treated sapwood on the outside has remained sound but the inner heartwood has completely decayed. When using the right hardwoods, the heartwood has excellent natural durability so it does not matter that there is only preservatives in that sapwood. The very centre, the heart, must not be exposed.

Sizes that might be considered are 200x200, 250x200, 300x200, 250x250 and 300x200. About the largest size that should be considered in hardwood is 400x200 but this will have significant amounts of sapwood which can cause the ends to tear.

Figure 20.   200x100 mm heart in timber in the process of becoming two pieces

Figure 21.   200x200 mm heart in timber with random split.

The larger sizes in hardwood require the designer to give thought as to when to exclude heart and when to permit it. The subject of heart in timber is very important for designers to understand and master as its inappropriate use can adversely impact aesthetics in a major way as illustrated in Figure 20 and Figure 21. Present standards for structural timber are far too generous in their allowance of heart in timber. The implications of inappropriately allowing heart in material is explained in considerable detail in my book, *The Seven Deadly Sins of Timber Design* and in summary is:

- Do not allow heart in timber in sizes where the smallest dimension is 175 mm, e.g. 300x150.
- Avoid specifying 150x150 mm as invariably it will contain heart.

For larger heart free sizes:

- Sizes up to 300x100 mm can be supplied heart free but in limited quantities and
- Place growth rings down on horizontal surfaces (natural feature permitting)[62].

Figure 22. Preferred growth ring alignment.

Note on Figure 22: While it is important to have a timber specification, it is important to have procedures in place to confirm that timber has been supplied to that grade. The image shows the correct growth ring alignment but the timber is cut too close to the centre of the tree and incorporates the less stable juvenile wood which has caused checking in the timber. This timber does not comply with any structural grade. Because the timber has been aligned the right way, the worst effects of the checking have been avoided.

Surface Finish

Pine will normally only be supplied with a micro reeded finish called "rougher headed." A micro reeded finish on pine will help mask and possibly even reduce any minor surface checking. As such it can provide some improvement in appearance, at least initially. Rougher heading is a worthwhile initiative on pine, but, as mentioned earlier, it will not save you from the impact of significant moisture cycling and the propagation of splits, particularly on horizontal surfaces. Apart from some initial appearance benefits it also seems to hold coating systems better because of the increased surface area and the ridges which ensure a good thickness.

---

[62] The presence of natural feature on the heart side may preclude the ideal alignment of the growth rings.

Hardwood can be supplied in a variety of finishes depending on the type of item being designed.

Figure 23.   Barbecue table made from rough sawn timber but table top is thicknessed.

Robust furniture. In locations, such as national parks (Figure 23), the legs and cross rails will normally be rough sawn but, also as mentioned, if working with jigs, the bottom of the rails should be sized at least for height. The horizontal surfaces in such furniture should be rough sawn but also coarse sanded. Rough sawn timber weathers far better than dressed timber giving a longer life and requiring less ongoing maintenance.

There is limited availability of planers that can dress or size very large sizes as most planers will be limited to 300x100 or 125 mm. Larger sizes may have to be either rough sawn or alternatively sanded or wire brushed.

Refined architectural pieces – except where a specialty finish is required, e.g. carving and surface texturing, all timber will be dressed all round

What sizes to use

Figure 24.   Wide thin boards are unstable.

When fully exposed, the resistance of horizontal members to cupping, even the most durable timber, will be dependent on its width to thickness ratio. A member 145x45 has a ratio of 3.2 to 1 and will give no problems but an unseasoned 145x35 which is 4.1 to 1 can be expected to cup. My experience is not to go beyond 3.5 to 1 for unseasoned and 4 to 1 for seasoned. Thin boards ex[63] 25mm and finished 19 mm or so after dressing can be unstable, particularly if wide as illustrated in Figure 24.

---

[63] The term "ex" is commonly used in the timber industry to denote the nominal unseasoned sawn size.

Another consideration is whether sawmill recovery sizes can be utilised. These are ex 50x25, 38x38, 50x50 and 75x38 mm. These sizes are normally chipped as they have little demand and, if sold, are usually sold for a low, noncommercial price. Utilising these sizes is very environmentally responsible but you will need to make arrangements with the miller to supply them. Be prepared to pay a price that is commensurate to the effort involved. The specification should mention a supplier and an anticipated lead time. Again evidence of ordering in time may be required.

Figure 25. These slats are sawmill recovery material.

4 Glued Timber

Occasionally, a kiln dried member size is desired in a size that is larger than the 42-45 mm thickness range that can be sourced commercially. It unwise to glue laminate timber for external use! This advice is, on the surface, contrary to an Australian Standard which covers this very likelihood. AS5067 Non-Structural Glued Laminated Timber specifically mentions these joints in external furniture and permits them when used in the most challenging hot and humid conditions.[64] The only real restrictions are that the moisture content is below 18% and the species being glued is of a service class appropriate to the intended use and service environment. In this Standard under "Performance and production requirements" it states that it "Specifies requirements for non-structural timber assemblies manufactured from timber laminate having grain direction parallel with each other and glued together to form a single unit." Appendices A and B of that standard specify methods for testing cleavage of glued joints and glueline shear, respectively. Appendix C provides guidelines for selection, production and installation of non-structural glulam.

So, while there is a standard that can be referenced to justify a glued joint, is that a wise course of action? Appendix C of the standard warns of the difficulty in achieving successful glued joints in externally exposed products saying:

> This appendix provides guidelines for the selection, production and installation of non-structural glulam meeting the performance requirements of this Standard. Although compliance with the recommendations contained herein will usually produce satisfactory non-structural glulam assemblies, complete documentation of all processes is not possible, and no warranty can be given by Standards Australia that this will actually occur. It is the responsibility of the specifiers, producers and users of non-structural glulam assemblies to select, manufacture, fabricate and install the product in such a way that it meets the performance requirements of this Standard. (Emphasis mine).

---

[64] Table 2.1

The glueing of joints on the legs and table top is a very similar process to making a structural laminated hardwood beams. Despite being made to higher standards in a very controlled environment, no experienced building designer would consider using them externally. The warranty would be void.[65] Successful gluing of Australian hardwoods is dependent on a number of factors which include:

- Ensuring the timber is dressed and had the adhesive applied and pressed all within 30 minutes
- Knowing the right pressure and gluing time for the temperature
- Knowing the peculiarities of the individual species including the pH.[66]
- Using an adhesive which provides some flexibility. The most common being resorcinol which does not give a clear glueline

IMAGE NOT AVAILABLE

Figure 26.   Failed glue joint in external furniture.

Clearly, glued joints have been and will continue to be an important part of internal furniture but their successful use in that application does not mean that they should be considered in external furniture. To ensure that glued joints are not built into the furniture by an over-enthusiastic fabricator the working drawings and the specifications should have a note that no glued joints are permitted. In the chapter on round timber, some guidance is given on achieving larger sections without using glued joints.

---

[65] For example Hyne's recommendations are "Shielding of the beam from free moisture or direct sun. The use of metal, fibro or plastic shields on the exposed faces or ends of beams is required to help maintain the beam in an unstressed dry condition. Technical Data Sheet 6, (No publication data May 14) 2.

[66] For example, Bootle suggests that tallowwood gluing surfaces may have to be treated with 10% sodium hydroxide prior to glueing. Bootle, Keith R. *Wood in Australia, Types Properties and Uses, Second Edition*. (McGraw Hill: Sydney, 1983) 350.

5 Round Timber

Round timber can be used in external furniture in three basic formats. The most sophisticated is when they are machined from square or rectangular kiln dried material, normally hardwood. The rounds could also be from true diameter pine thinnings where regular size makes commercial design and construction a possibility. The third option is using natural rounds in a variety of materials giving a rustic "bush carpentry" feel with one off creations.

Machined rounds up to 42 mm diameter

The final machined sizes for kiln dried sizes for hardwoods with shrinkage up to 6% are found in Table 3. Generally speaking we are talking about 31 mm finish for ex 38 mm unseasoned timber and 42 mm finish for ex 50 mm unseasoned. A few mills are cutting some oversized stock which finishes 35 and 45 mm respectively after machining but sourcing this material in rough sawn format for custom processing is not easy so, for all intents and purposes, can be ignored. Once tooling has been sourced, square timber can be turned into rounds quickly by the use of a dowel machine or through simply machining it like any other profile in a planer. Lathe work is impractical for large quantities of round dowel like material though for small quantities it may be the most economic option as tooling costs for dowel machines and planers can be high.

Machined rounds over 42 mm diameter.

Solid round members up to 65 mm must come from 75x75mm square whereas sizes between 66 to 89 mm are produced from 100x100 square. It is impossible to kiln dry these sizes commercially as they generally split due to the stresses involved. Air drying is not an option either as it takes about a year to dry every 25 mm thickness. Purchasing old, recycled timber is no guarantee that you will receive dry timber either. Timber that had come from sawn members in a demolished building will be dry but if it is cut from large round sections such as girders or powerpoles the timber will be unseasoned as the original member is simply too large to dry.

Larger diameter rounds are still achievable, either using a two-piece, non-glued construction or a single piece processed differently to allow quick seasoning with less danger of splitting. To explain how to do this I am using as examples 51 and 64 mm diameters.

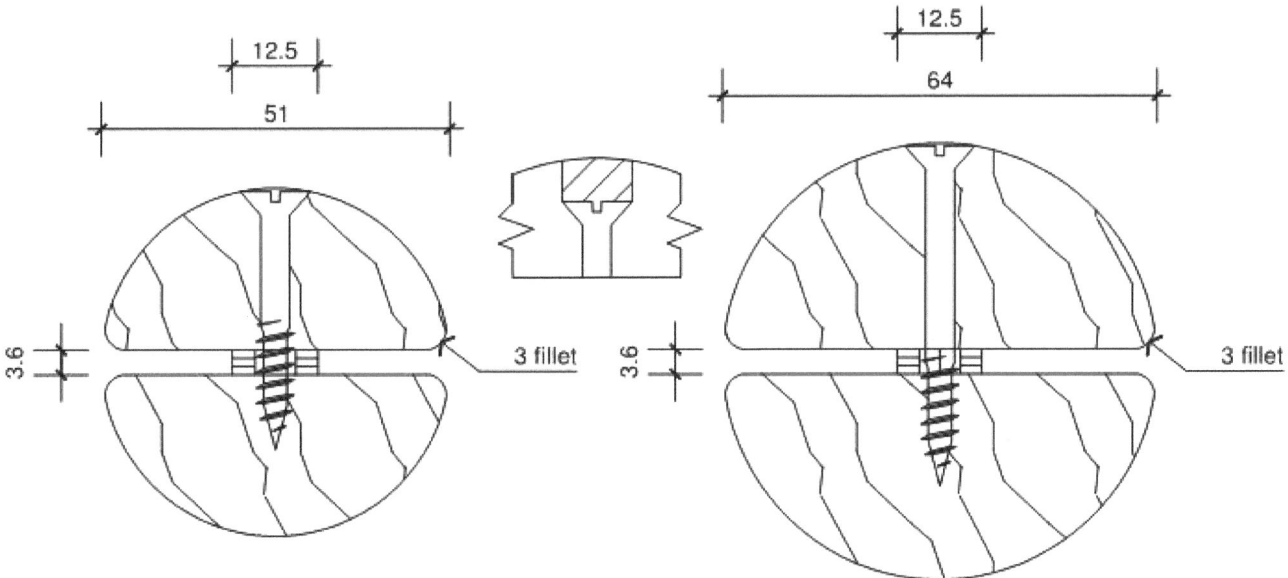

Figure 27. Two examples of round timber members fabricated from commercially available kiln dried timber sizes.

Two-piece construction is illustrated in Figure 27 allows the leg to be fabricated from ex 38 mm stock. The groove is even over the whole length unlike the failed glue-joint seen in Figure 26. Compared to what the option is, it presents an alternative but probably acceptable aesthetic because it looks as if it is intended to be there. The two-piece construction will require profiled cutters to be made but should be able to be manufactured relatively easily on a spindle moulder. The 3 mm fillet on the corners should prevent splinters.

It is envisaged that larger round members will be used as legs or other main items and making connections with round items can be difficult and frequently this is done with welded pipe frames. If this is the case the size of the washers used does matter (3 washers at 1.0 mm thick = 3 mm whereas if 1.5 mm it will be 4.5mm and then most likely not fit). The size of all the hardware and nominating a source where it can be purchased from is important.

Surface coatings are discussed in the chapter on finishings but it should be noted that the legs, if made from hardwood, should be pre-leached and coated on all faces prior to assembly.

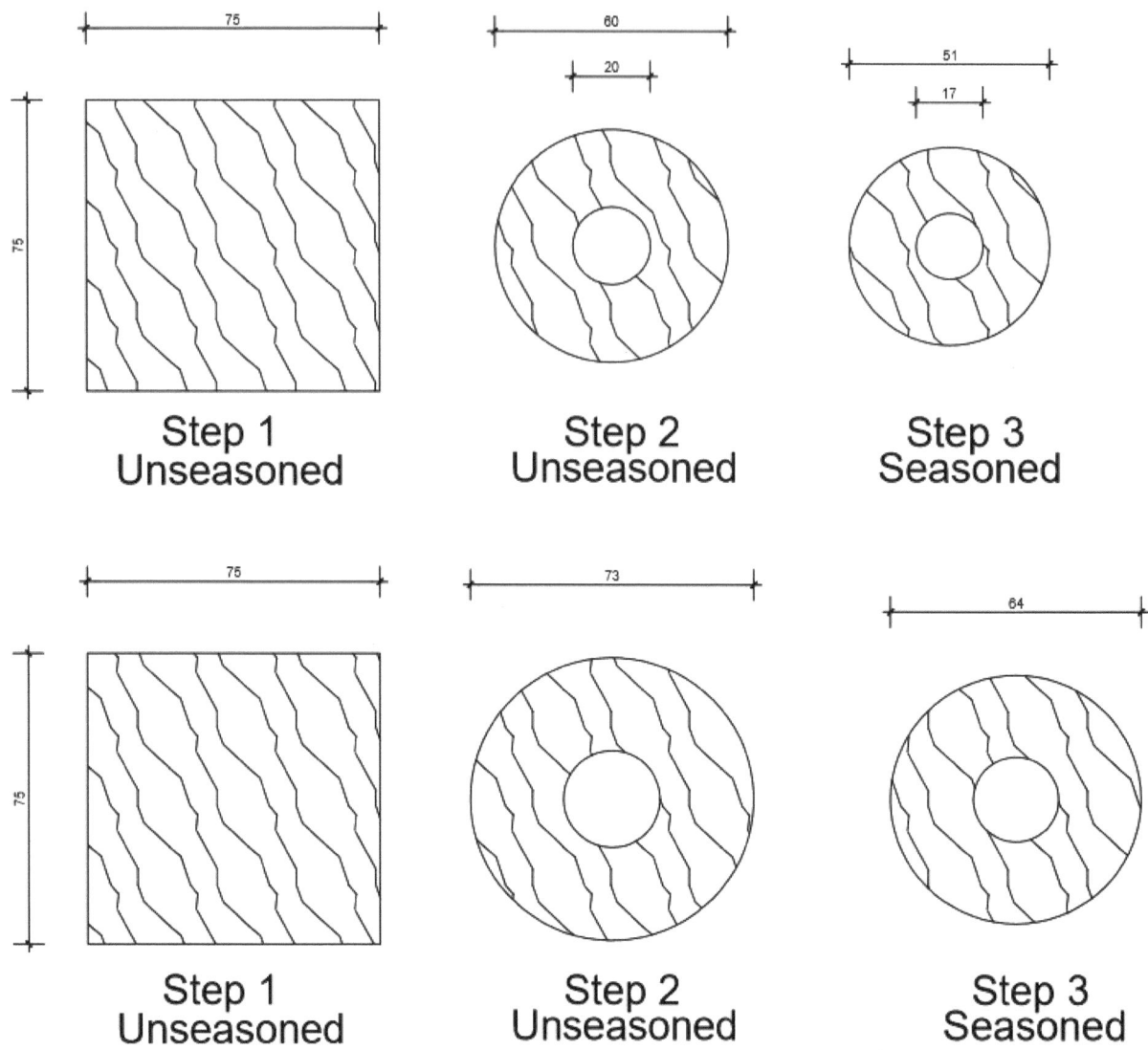

Figure 28. Producing larger rounds from solid piece.

A second option which gives different aesthetics is shown in Figure 28. Here a piece of green off saw 75x75 is turned down to either 60 or 73 mm and a hole, measuring roughly one third of the diameter, is drilled the full length of the piece. This allows seasoning from inside also instead of just the usual outside only. After drying, which is much more rapid and with far less stress, the timber is turned down to its final size. I have never seen this done in hardwood but this process was identified a long time ago as the solution to splitting on the face of pine posts. It would be reasonably expected to be as successful in hardwood as with pine.[67]

The advantage of option shown in Figure 27 is that kiln dried material may be ready to supply (depending on species) but it may be seen as having less desirable aesthetics. The disadvantage of option shown in Figure 28 is that lead time may be a minimum of 3 months but, arguably, has better

---

[67] As an example TTT Products in New Zealand produce it in products as large as powerpoles. URL: http://www.unilog.co.nz/product-31-ttt-multipoles--foundations. Date Accessed: October 2, 2017.

aesthetics.

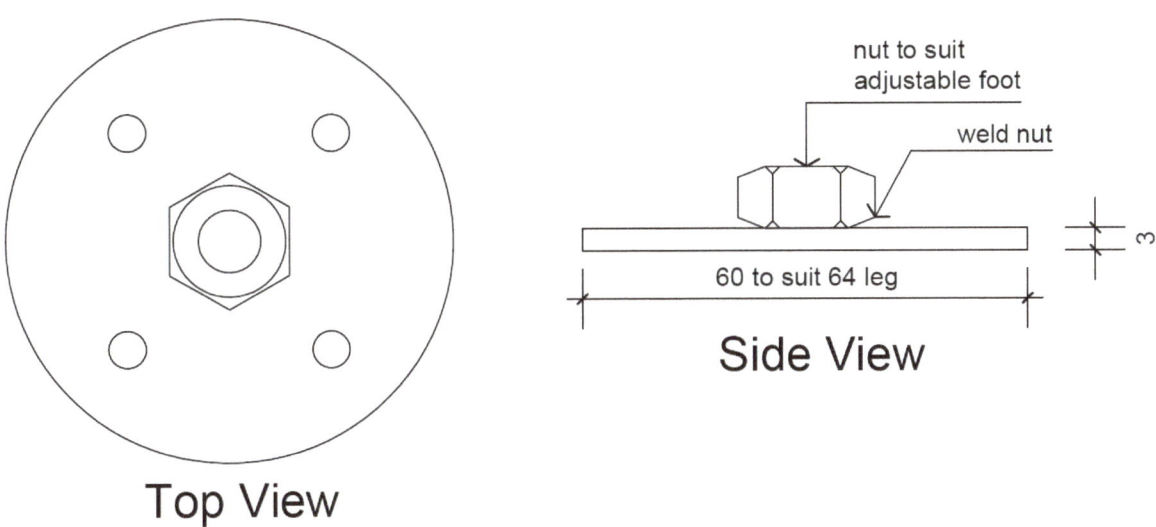

Figure 29.   Base plate for timber legs to accommodate adjustable leg.

Legs will require adjustable feet when the paving is uneven and both these options require a stainless plate screwed into the end grain of the legs, say 3 mm thick to allow for stainless countersunk screws. There should be a minimum of 4 screws say 8# x I". The plate should have a nut welded to the back to accommodate the thread on the adjustable feet – refer Figure 29.

Natural rounds

Figure 30.   Jimmy Possum style bush carpentry chair.

The "organic look", where small natural rounds are used instead of processed timber, steel or plastics, is becoming popular in children's playgrounds. The very irregularity of the timber is its attraction and simple bolted joints make them relatively easy to construct. Being installed in the ground gives them the rigidity needed. Our colonial bush carpentry tradition saw the effective use of even smaller diameter hardwood to create effective free standing furniture without any modern fasteners at all. Despite their rustic look they could be very sophisticated, and items such as the Jimmy Possum[68] chair (Figure 30) are built with joints that tightened when sat on. Recreating them in the 21st century is very expensive and the presence of sapwood made them unsuitable for long term fully weather exposed applications. Performance under a patio would be very acceptable. The small size of some of the members means that generally they are not suitable for areas where furniture needs to be robust. These will normally be purchased as proprietary items and the details of their design is not covered by this book. Lyctus attack is a possibility if the wrong species is used.

There is more acceptance of natural round timber furniture in the North American market and there are a

---

[68] Jimmy Possum was an enigmatic man, possibly aboriginal, who lived in a hollowed out tree in Tasmania and was a builder of bush furniture. His chairs from the 1890's to early 1900's are now collectors' items.

number of manufacturers who have highly mechanised plants for producing this type of furniture. The sizes used are far more robust however than those used in the chair illustrated in Figure 30.

The use of natural rounds, however, should not be dismissed out of hand as there is a place for them in more robust sizes as Figure 31 shows. Here segments of small logs are cut to length and used as seats and table supports. These natural rounds, even without treatment, will perform well under a patio in cypress and hardwood, provided the timber is not lyctus susceptible. Used fully in the weather the sapwood would either need to be removed (a must for cypress) or be treated.

Figure 31. Natural rounds used in a winery on the island of Cypress.

Machined pine rounds

Figure 32. These attractive internal seats highlight the difficulty in making connections with round timber.

While, in Australia, natural rounds are really only suited to a cottage industry because of the innate variability between components and the skill needed to manufacture them, machined rounds provide uniformity that suits commercial production. Making joints with round timber is always a problem but much of that difficulty can be removed by adopting a hole and spigot connection. Pine will need to be treated but caution will be needed to ensure that the timber is not treated with CCA. Treatment with CCA and ACQ or Tanalith E will not be distinguishable apart from the label on the end which will be removed during processing. Longitudinal splitting is a problem with pine rounds.

I have experimented making true diameter posts from untreated cypress, which would be ideal for this application also, and it was successful. Finding a supplier may be difficult though.

6 Detailing Frames and Fasteners

Using frames made from fabricated steel or aluminium can give improved aesthetics and considerable freedom in the design of external furniture. Castings are also used by a number of proprietary manufacturers but are not covered in this guide. The high cost of developing patterns for sand casting, let alone the vastly greater expense involved with dies for the better finish resulting from pressure casting, mean that large numbers have to be involved to recoup the outlay. As well, small changes are not feasible as this involves making costly tooling changes.

Figure 33. Fabricated galvanised steel frame. Note: Design is copyright to Guymer Bailey Architects and was manufactured under license by the author.

Figure 34. Seat built on a cast aluminium frame

Over the years of making landscaping to drawings prepared by others I would occasionally be presented with designs which utilised steel and screw sizes that simply did not exist except in the imagination of the designer. Wishful thinking in the past was not a desirable trait as ultimately it led to frustration. There has been a revolution in recent years in the way metal components are fabricated which now allows far more freedom. Even greater changes are forecast with ever increasing performance of additive manufacturing, otherwise known as 3D printing. This will allow for designs to flow seamlessly from computer to finished product without the constraints caused by fabrication.

Fabrication used to involve cutting from a limited range of standard sizes and shapes and then drilling or punching holes, welding and then sending away to a galvainiser. In practical terms the carrier often had to wait up to two hours at the plant and then, in a couple of days' time, come back, hoping that nothing is lost in the bottom of the vat, wait a couple more hours to pick up the goods and deliver them back. While the cost of mild steel was relatively low, the associated fabrication and handling costs could be very considerable. There is much merit in by-passing mild steel altogether for laser cut stainless. For a start it gives the flexibility for shape and size that you don't have with standard steel sizes. Elongated holes are as easy as round and curves pose no more problems than a straight line. When used in conjunction with computerised presses all that is needed at most is a minimal amount of welding, and perhaps polishing, to achieve a completed item ready to take the timber.

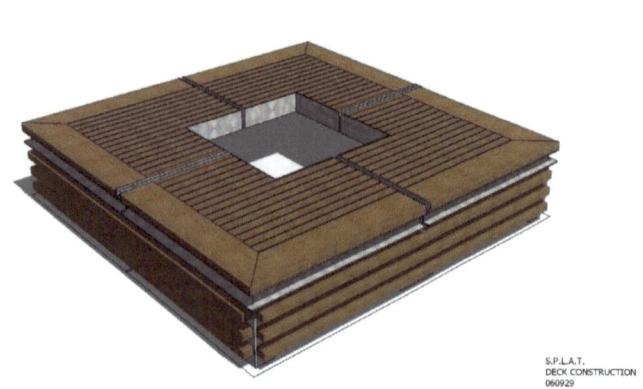

Figure 35.   A tree surround seat designed using standard steel sizes.

Each locality is going to have access to different equipment. A designer should acquaint him/herself with what is available but the requirements for outdoor furniture are generally not very onerous. You will need to ascertain:

- The thicknesses and grades of material available
- The maximum thickness that can be laser cut
- The maximum length and thickness that can be folded, and
- The amount of grip needed by the press.

Stainless can become very expensive if it has to be polished and for many applications it simply is not needed. If you would have been content with a galvanised finish then there is little point polishing, providing there are no environmental considerations such as salt air or pollution. In these situations there is little choice other than polished 316 grade but these situations would, of course, have meant that galvanising is not ideal either and extra attention would have been necessary. The designer will need to consider also if reflected light will also be an issue. A 2B finish is available in the thicker sizes that will be required. This finish is suitable for use "in some architectural applications that will not be closely examined for uniformity of finish such as downpipes and gutters".[69] Polishing does, however, reduce the possibility of tea staining. For brackets that are not visible my practice was to use 304 grade stainless and where visible, use 316.

---

[69] Australian Stainless Steel Development Association. *2B, 2D and BA Cold Rolled Finishes.* URL http://www.assda.asn.au/technical-info/surface-finishes/2b-2d-and-ba-cold-rolled-finishes. Date accessed. June 12, 2015.

3D printing as a rapid prototyping tool has been around for some years but 3D printing of actual products has only been a reality since 2008 and has only been taught in universities in Australia since 2010. One lecturer told how they had to pay $300000 for their first machine (and there are a number of different processes that can be used) but now it was possible to purchase an entry level machine for between $1000 and $2000, and these are machines that give a very credible performance. The required software that once cost tens of thousands of dollars is now available as freeware. Complexity, the enemy of normal manufacturing, does not come with any penalty. With the expiry of key patents relating to additive manufacturing, the cost of the machinery needed has reduced substantially but as yet, the key limiting factor has not been overcome, and that is speed. However, with very keen minds working on this, even that will be overcome. A designer should strive to keep abreast of developments in this field as, for younger professionals, it will become a reality.

Figure 36.   Complex bollard cap produced by 3D printing.

Suitable Fasteners

Screw durability was specified under AS 3566 Screws - Self-drilling - For the building and construction industries, which was introduced in 1988 in an attempt to counter the poor performance of imported fasteners particularly. Previously, compliance was to a material specification where products were deemed to comply if they had a certain coating thickness. The new standard adopted a stringent performance specification based on real life testing. For example, the test site for coastal use has to be "located less than 500 m from the mean high water line, in a coastal area with surf for most of the year".[70] Unfortunately this standard was withdrawn in 2015 though, at the time of writing, most suppliers are voluntarily complying with it. But the brand of screws allowed needs to be given more thought than before.[71] The Standard had four classes of corrosion resistance:

Class 1	For general internal use where corrosion resistance is of minor importance. Most ZINC/YELLOW drywall and chipboard screws are in this category.
Class 2	For general internal use where significant levels of condensation occur. Electroplated ZINC/YELLOW is generally used to meet this class.
Class 3	For general external use in mild industrial and marine applications. The class is intended for roofing and cladding screws in mild applications.
Class 4	For external use in marine and moderately severe corrosive environments, generally within 1 kilometre from marine surf, although topography and /or strong prevailing winds may extend this distance.
Table 6. Different classes of screws.[72]	

Issues of corrosion in zinc screws are well enough known to discount them immediately irrespective of the class they are given but why not galvanised or any Class 4 screw? Should you decide you are

---

[70] http://www.buildex.com.au/corrosion_management.html. Date accessed. June 7, 2015.

[71] As one manufacturer summed up the present situation, it is down to how much you trust the manufacturer's warranty.

[72] http://www.buildex.com.au/corrosion_management.html. Date accessed. June 7, 2015.

aiming for 50 years life as you should with domestic and industrial construction there seems little choice in the fasteners. In these instances they must be stainless steel (grade 304 or 316) as it is a simple matter of install and forget, but you will not achieve that extended time even with the very best hardwood, particularly horizontal pieces. One reputable manufacturer does say that their Class 4 screws are suitable for 50 years in a light industrial/urban application which most furniture installations will be.[73] There are two reasons for not using them:

- The need for maintenance. The manufacturer that gives the 50 year industrial/urban life has a requirement "that areas not exposed to rain should be washed down regularly. . . . Washing should be carried out at least every six months and more frequently in coastal areas and areas of heavy industrial fallout"[74]
- Whatever you specify has the danger of being substituted with a lower priced and hence the likelihood of a lower performing product.

Dissimilar materials are known to give corrosion issues so should stainless screws be used on a galvanised frame? There is very minimal corrosion with large areas of galvanised (as you would have in a frame) and stainless screws. There is significant corrosion when there is a large section of stainless and a galvanised screw.[75] There can be a problem when using class 4 self-drilling screws to attach the batten through a non-drilled galvanised frame as the less well corrosion protected shaft and black steel of the frame, and the swarf created through drilling, are in contact. Rust marks also can occur as a result of this practice. The steel frames should be predrilled prior to galvanizing to avoid this. In the event that the assembler is faced with having to drill the holes, a wipe of non-acid cure silicone in the hole should help.[76]

Bolts, unlike screws, are not a performance based product. In my book, *Timber Joints,* I write about and illustrate the deteriorating performance of imported galvanised bolts and the potential lack of effective corrosion resistance even with well galvanised bolts. For this reason I urge designers to specify stainless bolts.

---

[73] http://www.buildex.com.au/climaseal4.html. Date accessed. June 7, 2015.
[74] http://www.buildex.com.au/buildex_warranty.html. Date accessed. June 7, 2015.
[75] Collinson, Dave. Technical Manager, Buildex ITW. *Pers. Com.* April 2015.
[76] Bailey, Ralph. *Pers Com.* 13 March 2018.

When fastening to a metal frame, screwing from underneath is preferred (Figure 37) as shrinkage in thickness is then not an issue. Generally 14# screws will suffice. The holes in the frames should, ideally, be slotted to accommodate shrinkage. If using the 14# screw the hole would be 6.5 mm wide and sufficiently long in the slot to accommodate say 5 mm shrinkage if dealing with a 150 mm unseasoned board. (6% shrinkage on 150 mm is 9 mm/ and divide that by two for each fastener and the answer is 4.5 mm – say 5 mm.). With unseasoned timber, the screw is placed at the outer extremity and with seasoned timber place the screw in the centre of the elongated hole. Given the declining level of professionalism among many trades, it would be prudent to specify this on your plans.

Figure 37. Table top screwed to steel frame from underneath.

Consideration should also be given to using tamper resistant fasteners. The fasteners in Figure 38 while being high quality 316 stainless are easily vandalised without much effort. A simple shifting spanner will suffice. If there is any shrinkage in the timber the nut can be removed without any tools at all. The other problem that this image highlights is the potential for injury to clothing and should someone fall against them serious damage can result. Screws would have been a better option and ideally a screw with a tamper resistant head. A wide range of proprietary screws is available.

Figure 38. These fasteners are easily removed and can cause injury.

Painting Steel Supports

Figure 39. Rust coming through frame after six months.

Figure 40. Blooming on galvanised and powder coated steel.

If you choose to paint any steel supports you must be careful in specifying the coating. The purpose of the coating has to be clearly understood as some are purely decorative while others provide the primary and only means of corrosion resistance. Whatever top coat is chosen, as with the timber finishes, it is important to obtain the manufacturer's recommendations for preparation and undercoating which must be followed.

Decorative finishes

I built a bridge once where the handrails were specified "galvanised and powder coated black" which is exactly what I did. It looked impressive when first built but I soon had a claim from my customer who was upset at the white blooming on the balustrades, refer Figure 40. The application was not far from the sea and I quickly discovered that these situations needed a very expensive specialty powder coated finish. The same disappointing result can occur on external furniture situated close to the coast due to pinholing that can exist with unsuitable powder coating.. Having learnt a very costly lesson, I would in future seek a written specification from a reputable paint manufacturer as to the best process and product to use in a given location. Powder coating (and other coatings over galvanizing) has its own problems and some manufacturers don't recommend it.

Corrosion Resistant Finishes

Primary corrosion resistance can be achieved through a painted finish. Far from being a second best option, corrosion resistance equal to galvanised is possible with a suitable paint, and even better resistance in a marine environment. We have found a two coat epoxy siloxane system[77] excellent for these purposes but even then our practice is to put a sacrificial coating between the timber and the paint. This is because of the extractives, acidity of the timber and treatments. During design, consider how you can touch up the paint as it may get damaged during transit and erection. Consider, also how to maintain the steel during a major refurbishment after many years. Can it recoated in situ? It must also be able to be repaired with a paintbrush and not sent back to the paint shop as can be the case with powder coating and some paint finishes.

---

[77] As we have been thanked by customers for introducing them to the product we use, I have no hesitation mentioning it here by name. The product we use is PPG's PSX700 which is derived from a paint produced to withstand the marine environment and intense heat of rocket launches at NASA's Cape Canaveral. The two coat system utilises an epoxy zinc rich primer (or other primers if required) for primary anti-corrosive protection, followed by the polysiloxane which also provides anticorrosive qualities as well as very high gloss, and long term colour retention as required for topcoats. This system meets and exceeds the requirements of ISO 12944-6 C5-M High. This system provides corrosion protection to first maintenance of greater than fifteen+ years. When choosing a paint system you should be specifying to ensure performance that matches this product.

7 Detailing Timber Components

Our political masters constantly remind us that "The devil is in the detail" and this is strongly the case with external furniture. Everything is working against long term satisfactory performance but it can be achieved when careful attention is given to the fine details of the design. This chapter deals with observations I have made about correct detailing as well as poor design that can adversely impact upon performance.

Drawings

"Preliminary" drawings are appropriate to show the client during the design stage to explain the architectural intent and when you are seeking feedback and things are in a state of flux. When more refined they are also suitable during any approval process with councils etc. Only after all parties are satisfied with what is proposed should a "For Construction" edition be issued. If this practice is not followed there is a danger of two different construction drawings being in circulation. The author has encountered this problem personally. "Preliminary" drawings are not suitable for construction drawings!

The "For Construction" drawings should leave nothing to the fabricators imagination. If you imagine a 14# stainless steel screw and don't specify it, a cheaper 8# screw, zinc plated is likely to be used. If you imagine high quality decorative timber of a certain species but don't have a tight specification you will have a low grade lower durability framing timber. Similarly with paint and oil finishes. The problems that are encountered with external furniture are all solvable at the design stage. Until the plans are issued the drawings are just lines on paper and can be easily changed. Welcome input from experienced specialists but be cautious as not all "specialists" fully understand what they are doing. They may be used to producing to a price rather than to a specification and performance requirement.

Fastening horizontal members

Figure 41.   Horizontal members secured to 75 mm wide supports

Figure 42.   Split 50 mm support on a barbecue table.

When designing robust furniture it is common practice simply to screw, usually with a 14# batten screw, the horizontal members to a timber frame. The same problem occurs as with decking to joists. If a 50 mm wide support is used then the screws must be in a straight line and so, as a result, split the member. Moisture then enters and degrade eventually occurs. When 75 mm supports are used, a stagger of at least 16 mm can be achieved and this will usually avoid splitting providing the timber is predrilled. Pine is probably not as prone to splitting as the hardwood but the possibility should be considered in the design. Using a 75 mm hardwood support means that the support is unseasoned. A 70/75 mm wide pine support will not be available. Under no circumstance should a hexagonal head screw be used to face fix timber as this will require countersinking and promote decay through water pooling.

Figure 43. Using a double 50 mm support to prevent splitting.

Figure 44. Fastening from underneath to a timber frame.

Two ways of using 50 mm supports are shown in Figure 43 and Figure 44. They would be suitable with either kiln dried or green off saw supports. The double support of Figure 43 allows for one screw in each rail and the distance between the next screw is sufficiently large to avoid splitting. By far the best method of securing the horizontal members is by using a bracket from underneath (Figure 44) which also allows a considerable degree of prefabrication and ease of transport. When fastening from underneath, both shrinkage and weathering of the timber around the top countersink are no longer a consideration.

As mentioned in the chapter on frames, when fastening from underneath, it is prudent to use slotted holes whether the timber is kiln dried or not for the timber is still going to expand and contract. With unseasoned timber, the screw is placed at the outer extremity and with seasoned timber place the screw in the centre of the elongated hole. Given the declining level of professionalism among many trades, it would be prudent to specify this on your plans.

Figure 45.   This seat has the ideal fixing detail

The seat from the UK shown in Figure 45 has, in my opinion, the ideal fixing arrangement for timber to a metal frame. The boards, all bar one, are narrow and only require one central fastening meaning shrinkage/expansion is never an issue. It will work as well with unseasoned as with seasoned timber. The fastenings are also from behind but what makes this fixing superior is that the timber is spaced away from the frame and so reducing the amount of contact and therefore minimizing moisture entrapment. This can have a significant impact on the timber life under certain circumstances. A simple 6 mm thick galvanised steel washer will suffice.

Housed joints

When traditional styles of external furniture are required, it is not always possible to avoid housed joints but they are not desirable as they trap moisture and promote decay. The seat in Figure 46 is representative of commonly available flatpack external furniture constructed using housed joints which have no weather protection at all. This type of seat is available, at time of writing, for prices that start from under $200.[78] While the designs are traditional, they also traditionally would have been used in the milder climates of the UK and Europe. They would have also been made in timber durable for the climate. Furniture made from fast grown rose gum from a South American plantation can be expected to quickly exhibit decay in the joints.

Figure 46.   Traditional seat with housed joints

When deciding whether to use an off the shelf item, the designer must explore carefully what species is being used as well as the robustness of the joint. When a number of items are required, With the ready availability of CNC routers, it is prudent to consider having them made specially to ensure the most durable species are used.

Painted pine, subject to the recommendations of this guide, is also an option in these applications providing the preservation of the timber is undertaken after all machining and drilling but before assembly. This is an application ideally suited to LOSP if the quality of treatment can be ensured.

---

[78] At the time of writing, one online retailer Temple and Webster was selling a three person seat made from "eucalyptus timber" for $189 and had prices as low as $149.

Occasionally, housed joints will be required in robust furniture. The seat in Figure 47 is built on a 100x100 mm post which, as it is an inground application, is ironbark. Even after housing the seat support into the frame there is still a generous amount of timber and significant degrade is not expected. Note that in this design, the diagonal brace which bears on the post near ground level is not housed as the extra moisture at this point could be a problem.

Figure 47.   Housed joint in robust furniture.

IMAGE NOT AVAILABLE

IMAGE NOT AVAILABLE

Figure 48.   Housed joint - view from top.

Figure 49.   Housed joint – view from underneath.

Normal furniture construction such as the housed joint on the perimeter trim of the table seen in Figure 37, Figure 48 and Figure 49 can trap moisture and lead to decay in the joint. In situations such as this the designer must consider alternate detailing that achieves the same effect. In this case the trim could have been attached to the table with stainless steel plates with countersunk screws.

Slope of grain

Once the designer moves away from straight pieces to items that are shaped, consideration needs to be given to the slope of the grain. The edge trim shown in Figure 50 clearly illustrates how the slope of the grain goes from being in line with the piece to being approximately at a 45 degree angle making it very easy for the timber to fracture.

Figure 50. Excessive slope of grain.

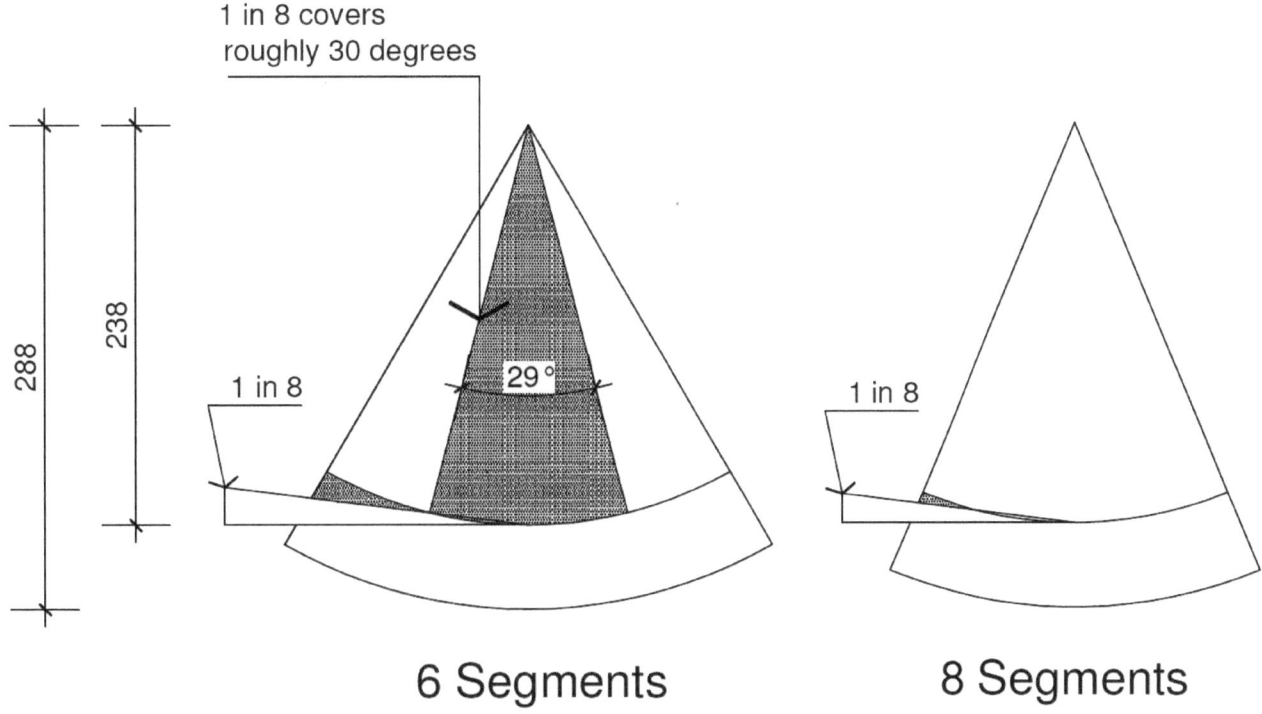

Figure 51. How slope of grain changes with the perimeter of a round table. Note that the triangle represents a slope of 1 in 8. And the associated shaded area represents the area beyond 1 in 8.

Figure 52. Round table without external trim avoids moisture entrapment and slope of grain issues.

The difficulty in keeping the slope of grain at an acceptable level on a round table should cause a designer to seriously consider the suitability of using such a trim.

Corners

A square cut corner member without any rounding over presents an unacceptable risk in the event of anyone falling against it – hardwood in particular. Arrising of corners is a minimum requirement. The table in Figure 53 has generous 100x100 mm mitres on the seats and top and, for added protection, the top of each board has a 3 mm radius all round which again is a minimum requirement.

Figure 53. This table has mitred and pencil rounded corners.

Figure 54. Failed mitre on table trim.

Figure 55. Mitre filled with debris and expanding.

Perimeter trims on rectangular furniture are much easier than on round as slope of grain is not a consideration but the corners particularly can still give trouble. In Figure 54 a neat internal cabinetry style glued joint was attempted. This joint would have given no trouble internally and even possibly been satisfactory for some time on a patio but failed spectacularly when fully weather exposed. The mitre in Figure 55 is not glued but detritus from the site has entered into the join, got wet and expanded forcing the top outwards over time. I have observed this particularly as being a problem where sand is involved. Both joints would have been better and trouble free if they did not touch but had say a 5 mm gap between the two pieces. This small gap would not have been a finger entrapment while allowing movement as in the case of Figure 54 and not allowed a buildup of material as in Figure 55.

Contacting the ground

Figure 56. Hardwood Posts separated from the ground

Figure 57. Pine posts separated from the ground

Moisture enters the end grain of timber approximately eight times faster than through the side grain. This means that when the furniture is in contact with the ground it can, in time, decay at the end. When the table is intended to be moved there is nothing that can be done other than use a high durability timber, ideally an In Ground Durability 1 species such as ironbark. When the tables are fixed in position the opportunity exists to raise the ends of the timber a little above the ground on metal supports. Compare Figure 9 with a later version of the same table seen in 0 where the earlier table is simply set in concrete.

Overhang and distance between supports

Unsupported timber, particularly rectangular sizes up to 50 mm thick, laid on the flat is prone to movement and, as odds will have it, one board will move upwards and the adjacent board will move downwards compounding what might otherwise have been visually acceptable. The length of overhang should ideally be limited to 150 mm as, beyond this, movement will become noticeable. I readily concede this is not practical in many instances so a tie will need to be introduced under the overhanging boards. This can be a piece of timber or galvanised or stainless steel. Refer to Figure 23 where the overhang is partly responsible for the timber's instability.

Figure 58. The overhang on this disabled access is tied together with a 75x6 mm stainless plate underneath.

The distance between the legs also needs consideration and, for the same reason, usually a centre tie is also needed. Timber will stay straighter if it is tied in three places. Unsupported or untied spans should not exceed 800 mm.

Detailing furniture containing large section timbers

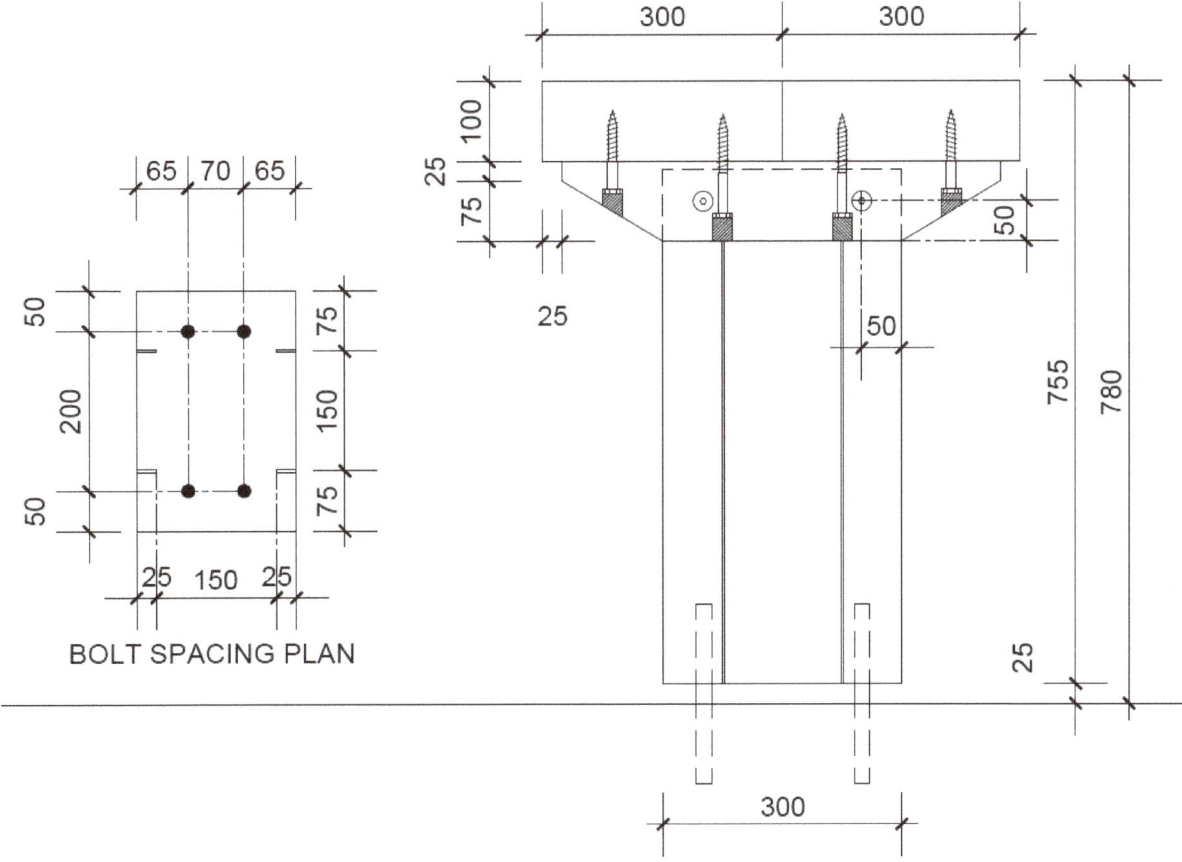

Figure 59. Table using large size members. No gap at construction of table to minimise the gap. Posts are 300x200 mm, twin rails 100x50 mm, top 300x100 mm. Bolt spacing plan is the bottom of post – note expansion groove.

An example of using large section timber can be seen in Figure 60 where the seats and table top are made from 300x100 mm heart free spotted gum. The posts in this case are a regular size 100x100 mm, again heart free. Fastening is from underneath which is preferred. A different table arrangement can be seen in Figure 59 where the support post is 200x300 mm. This is a size that cannot be supplied heart free. This size timber will normally split badly down one face but this is easily avoided by forming two anti-split grooves on each of the wider faces. The grooves in are 3 mm wide and 25 mm deep. (Refer to Figure 59 for a typical example of the groove placemen). Instead of tearing down one face the timber will move on the saw cut, either opening or closing. It is very important that

Figure 60. Barbecue table using chunky 300x100 mm spotted gum horizontal members. Note that access is not ideal.

these cuts be formed very soon after the timber has been milled as this splitting can occur very soon after sawing.

The heart allows moisture to enter the timber up to eight times faster than through the side grain. To avoid any long term degrade of the heart, the end of the timber in Figure 59 is kept 25 mm above the ground. The weakness of the detailing is that there is no provision in the attachment of the tops and seats to the support frame to allow for shrinkage. The holes should be elongated about 5 mm.

Detailing large section freestanding pieces

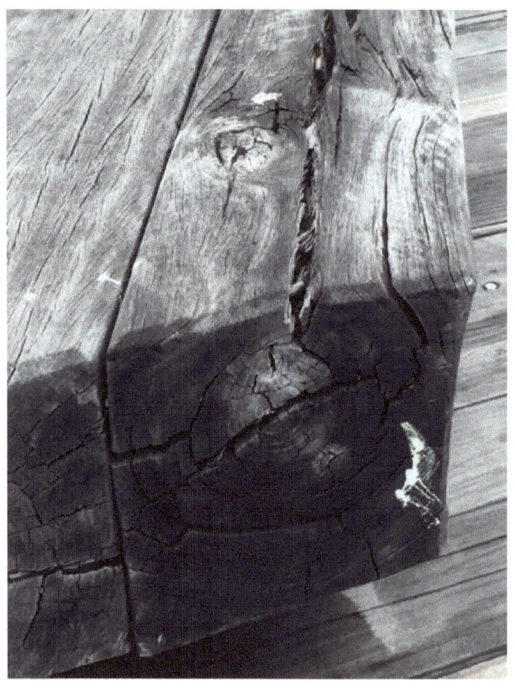

It can be unusual for large free standing pieces such as 300x300 mm heart in seats to be successful in the long term. This is not a problem with the resource as such, as they are generally not detailed in a way that accommodates the different properties of heart in timber and that which is heart free. Some of these seats can even be dangerous as poor detailing can allow finger entrapments to develop (Figure 61). But heart in material is a good resource providing you work with its limitations. So how do you detail this material?

Figure 61. 300x300 seating splitting along one face.

Figure 62. 300x300 mm seat when first installed

Figure 63. Vertical bolting has led to serious degrade after 13 years.

The designer of the 300x300 mm seating in Figure 64 has correctly detailed the way they are bolted to the deck. Frequently they are bolted through the top for ease of construction but this allows moisture into the heart which can cause early degradation (refer Figure 62 and Figure 63).

Figure 64.   Side bolting

With large sawn sizes, the outside is losing moisture and shrinking but the centre is retaining its moisture and so staying the same size. Something has to give, so it tears down at least one of the faces. The seat in Figure 61 has the heart off centre and it has been placed with the shortest distance to the heart uppermost and that is where it is splitting. The same with the seats in Figure 64, where splitting is to the surface closest to the heart. Good practice would see the heart placed closest to the underside. There is no obligation under AS 2082 to cut the material with the heart in the centre but it is none the less poor sawing not to attempt to have it central. But good practice alone is not going to ensure there will be no or very minimal splitting.

Figure 65.   Locating the heart centrally does not eliminate splitting

In Figure 65, the heart is in the centre of the three pieces but splitting still occurred. Ultimately the only way to prevent splitting is by the use of expansion grooves. On a 200 mm face you only need one but on a 300 mm you may and probably do need two. As mentioned earlier, the technique I used was to make the groove 25 mm deep and 3 mm wide. For the top surface it is wise to also arris the top of the groove (and also for all sides if used as posts). The gaps open and close as needs be and any tear is below the saw cut. These expansion grooves need to be cut very soon after milling – ideally within one week of milling.

Figure 66. Two only 400x200 mm hardwood used as seating. Custom anti split plates are used. Note anti skateboard notches

Figure 67. These pieces were left for too long prior to processing and plating and have started to split. Sapwood is evident on the outsides of the 400 mm dimension

When using very large sections such as 400x200 (which is about as large a piece of Australian hardwood as you can achieve) the tension in the sapwood is likely to cause the timber to tear down both sides of the wide face (Figure 67). Very soon after milling the expansion grooves should be formed and an additional plate secured to the end. My practice was to use 3 or 4 mm 316 stainless plate and attach it with 10 mm stainless coachscrews (Figure 66). The plate needs to be undersize of the timber cross section to allow for shrinkage – say 10% and the holes need to be slotted.

Figure 68. "Pole Cat" type nailplates should not be used on furniture

The ends should not be plated with "Pole Cats",[79] which are round or hexagonal nailplates intended to stop the heads of powerpoles splitting prior to installation. They are only lightly galvanised, and are forced out of the ends of the timber through the wetting and drying. This exposes very sharp edges. They can be used if there is a cap over the "Pole Cat".

---

[79] This product was developed by the author who held the registered design.

8 Leaching and Finishes

Weather exposure leads to premature degradation of the timber surfaces through the effects of UV and water absorption. It is important to consider whether a coating system should be used to protect your investment and what are the implications ongoing maintenance. Inappropriate or poorly maintained finishes can cause exterior furniture to deteriorate more rapidly than if there had been no coating at all. Checking, cracking, delaminating, discoloration, twisting and bowing can be minimised by correctly caring for your external furniture. Ttimber coatings do not necessarily improve the timber's resistance to decay and can, in fact, increase the risk substantially as they can reduce the ability of the timber to dry out. On the other hand, an appropriate finish should minimise weathering and the potential for fungal organisms to develop on the surface if there is any moisture.

The expected aesthetics will also impact finish choices. The horizontal surfaces of a hardwood barbecue table in a rustic national park setting, made from robust sizes of durable species will give over 20 years' service without any finishes ever being applied. In this setting, function, durability and vandal resistance are the primary considerations. However, these members are much larger than we would normally use in architectural high spec applications where a more refined look is required.

When considering coatings, the related matter of leaching of hardwood must also be considered.

Robust public furniture

Hardwood

Figure 69.   Robust barbecue table in a national park.

The barbecue table in Figure 69 was built to the standard New South Wales national parks' design. Durability is achieved through using hardwood species of high durability and of high quality. Sapwood must still be treated. The timber used is unseasoned as kiln drying would be pointless and, with the legs, impossible. The table is robust and during its lifetime could expect no more maintenance than a few coats of decking oil, if that. Should the timber start to look "tired", a simple sand with an angle grinder or belt sander will normally rejuvenate it. That is not to say that the tables should not be oiled but that if it is done it should be on a regular programmed basis. Moisture is the enemy of any timber and, while ever it has a coating that repels it, the associated degradation is minimised substantially.

With even the best hardwood about 3-5% of the boards may experience "shelling out", the term used to describe delamination of the growth rings. Shelling out will result in sharp splinters on the surface and will normally start occurring in the first six months. The table can be made safe by simply grinding out the affected areas if slight or replacing the whole board if necessary. Kiln drying does reduce the incidence of shelling out, probably halving it but does not completely eliminate it. Oil will not assist with this problem but placing boards with the growth rings down might.

Pine

Much public furniture is built from pine which must be treated to achieve any durability. When treated correctly, the preservatives used are effective in stopping decay but they, in themselves, are not effective in stopping the effects of wetting and drying. This can cause pine to, in effect, self-destruct. Without constant maintenance, performance can be unsatisfactory. One major manufacturer of pine furniture recommends reoiling twice annually as a minimum.[80] A lower maintenance alternative is to paint.

When pine furniture is kept under a roof (Figure 70) there is little difference in performance between it and hardwood.

Figure 70. Pine barbecue setting under a roof is giving good service

Refined Architectural Pieces

At the other end of the spectrum is external furniture used in applications such as restaurants. In these applications aluminium is not uncommon because of its cost and functionality but it also shouts "budget." Timber can be chosen in these applications for its beauty and improved ambience but the tradeoff is increased initial cost though justifiable considering the potentially long life of the furniture.[81] The hidden cost that needs to be factored in when considering this type of furniture is maintenance of the surface coatings. There are two options, clear film finishes and penetrating oils. Before one of these two options are chosen, the designer must consider whether the tannins will need to be leached.

---

[80] Landmark. *Maintenance Guide Document SLF 002-2.* (Landmark Products. Deception bay: UD) 1.
[81] As an example, the spotted gum furniture at the Opera Bar at the Sydney Opera House which was replaced after 18 years of service and then recycled into other venues run by the same group.

Leaching of Tannins

The issue of tannin bleed has to be considered in the design. All Australian hardwoods leach tannins, as do imported rainforest timbers. There is no leaching from pine or cypress. Some species, like kwila/merbau and blackbutt, produce large amounts of extractives while, spotted gum probably produces the least. (Combined with its durability, this is another good reason for choosing this species.) Figure 71 shows some kiln dried screening supplied by the author to a project in Japan when he was a novice at producing specialised timbers. The architect thought that if the timber was kiln dried

Figure 71. And then it rained! Spotted gum battens in Japan.

there would be no leaching and, sadly, I did not know any better at that time. I soon learnt otherwise as the first time it rained tannin stains ran down the white stonework. Similarly, with your furniture you have to consider if leaching will be an issue. Normally, in a park setting it is not but will be in a commercial application.

Figure 72. Blackbutt leaching onto concrete.

Even when the timber is "sealed" tannin can still be an issue. Three coats of a high quality decking oil will not prevent leaching, even on spotted gum. Oiling unseasoned timber, which anything above 50 mm has to be, is not as successful as would be hoped. The oil simply cannot penetrate when the timber is still filled with moisture. Film finishes can even degrade from the inside out due to the effect of the extractives.[82] One manufacturer requires a four to six week weathering period prior to applying their coating or having the timber pre-leached.[83] By leaving an extended period of time between installation and finishing, you would expect to have a problem from leaching if it rains over this period and it makes sealing all around impossible in some applications. Best practice in sealing requires the timber be coated all around, not just the visible face.

---

[82] Damien McTague, Woodmans Timber Finishes. *Pers. Com.* April 19, 2001.
[83] Intergrain. *Dimension 4 Ultra Primer*. URL: http://www.intergrain.com.au/product-selector/product-detail/intergrain-ultraprimer. Date accessed. 29 October 2017.

Specifying recycled timber does not prevent leaching. The timber may have been in service for 100 years but, if cut from larger sections such as girders and power poles, it will behave exactly the same as green off saw timber. It will generally not be seasoned[84] and will leach in the same way. Even old hardwood from a house demolition can be expected to leach as it has been protected from the weather. In building construction, one way of dealing with leaching is to ensure the tannins drip onto gardens or grass where it will not matter. This is generally not an option with external furniture. Timber can be pre-leached using proprietary products and these can be very effective.[85] It does not totally remove the possibility of leaching but it does make it more manageable. When timber has been pre-leached it is also more able to receive penetrating oils. The oxalic acid based proprietary products used to leach timber will also effectively remove tannin stains from concrete.

Figure 73.   Pre-leaching timber.

Film Finishes

Figure 74.   Decay under clear film finish.

A great deal of caution needs to be taken when choosing a film finish. While they can be made to work, the high cost of appropriate maintenance means that it is something that has to be discussed with the customer and an estimation of the cost should be known.

The table in Figure 74 illustrates spotted gum, the ends of which have severely degraded under the clear finish. There are marine varnishes available which are normally applied to areas which aren't heavily trafficked or used such as ship's handrails. Furniture would normally be considered in this category. Because these films are usually porous, moisture can enter and be trapped under the film so promoting degrade as is the case in Figure 74. Typical maintenance would be to sand the surface back to bare wood and then re-apply a new coat. Re-application over the top of an existing coating can cause serious problems especially if there is already a break in surface which may not be visible. The effect of trapped moisture then becomes apparent.

---

[84] Refer to the project Tree of Knowledge in my book *Architectural Timber Battens*.
[85] I have had success using Intergrain powerPrep followed by Intergrain Reviva.

Paint

The use of paint should not be discounted as a finish. It is not just a cheap alternative to using painted steel or aluminium. As one architect observed, "it still has a very timber look ,. . . [and] always looks different to fibre cement or metal".[86] Paint is a very reasonable choice of finishes especially now that we can see manufacturers warranting their product for unheard of lengths of time. One manufacturer warrants the paint for as long as you live in the house while another mentions 100 seasons.

What is causing the change in paint? As one surface coatings research chemist said, "They are finally pulling their head out of the sand regarding the variability of timber".[87] Considering the difficulties with timber, the following all impact on the success:

- high to low amounts of extractives
- high to low pH
- high to low shrinkage on unseasoned timber (13 to 3 %)
- continual dimension change with moisture content change
- surface finishes from rough to smooth
- high to low densities
- back sawn or quarter sawn
- great variability in absorption and
- great variability in grain characteristics.

The wonder is that paint succeeds at all with the stresses this variability can impose!

Generally, you cannot go wrong if you follow the manufacturer's recommendations. This is not always the case with paint. Let me explain. Some time ago, I built a truss bridge with painted 50x38 mm balustrades. I had the local sheltered workshop paint them and we used a premium acrylic gloss over a water based primer as was instructed on the can. We left them on a rack for a few days and then stacked them to return to our site. They all glued together and when separated, tore off paint. I called the representative of that paint company and he said that I used the wrong primer. Notwithstanding what was written on the can, I should have used an oil based primer. So much for labels. Even now we could be excused for being a little confused when determining the correct primer as different manufacturers specify differently. In Table Five, I give in summary form the recommendations of four different paint manufacturers for primers on external acrylic paint.

---

[86] Mainwaring, John. *Pers. Com.* April 27, 2015
[87] My source would rather not be named.

Dulux Weathershield Gloss	Wattyl Solagard Ultra Premium Low sheen	Taubmans Sunproof Exterior	Accent SolarMax
Self-priming on timber[88]	"If painting with white and white tone colours on a tannin rich timber, apply an initial coat of Solagard® as a sealer"[89]	"Tannin rich timbers should be primed with Taubmans Prep Right Wood Primer or Taubmans 3 in 1."[90]	"Where a primer is not specified apply three coats to previously unpainted surfaces"[91]

Table 7. Different priming instructions for acrylic paints.

My unfortunate experience with gluing from block stacking, though reduced next time around, was not solved by changing to an oil based primer. The issue was block stacking, not primers as the flexibility and permeability of the paint needed to withstand the variability of timber is exactly the reason the balustrades glued together. But what is the right primer - water, oil or no primer at all? Regardless of the recommendations above, all these manufacturers produce a primer suitable for these paints and what are we to make of a guideline suggesting a primer "may" be specified?

A primer is used to provide a strong bond between the wood and successive coats. It functions as a sealer and a water repellant, sometimes with fungicides added and is formulated to have a dull finish to aid with the adhesion of the top coats. When we first started selling paint, the sales representative told us, "Oil and water do not mix, so do not use an oil primer under a water based top coat". It sounds logical but it was incorrect as oil based primers are frequently used under water based paints. Timber Queensland is more specific in their advice relating to cladding which is similar to external furniture in the terms of risk. They say, "For all cladding where a painted finish is required, boards **should** (emphasis mine) be **primed all round** (emphasis mine) with a solvent (oil) based primer plus one coat of undercoat, colour matched to the final finishing coat. This will ensure that significant colour variations will not be apparent due to any shrinkage or movement that may occur later. Knots in hardwood may be sealed with a two pack polyurethane, a proprietary specialty finish or other sealer recommended by the paint manufacturer".[92] Sealing the knots in pine is essential. A primer, most likely oil based, should be part of your paint specification.

What type of paint should you use? In 2006 Timber Queensland advised, "Solvent borne (alkyd or oil) finishes are more resistant to water vapour than water borne (acrylic) finishes. Where a high level of protection is required, a finish system with a solvent borne primer and/or undercoat should be selected". While acknowledging the easier application and the improvements in water based paints, the objection was that "softer films tend to retain more dirt than alkyd (solvent based) paints, and thus harbour more mold growth".[93] Despite big advances in paint technology, they saw no reason to revise that recommendation in the March 2014 review of their recommendations. Against this, there are now water based enamels that are promising, at least through accelerated weathering trials, to match the

---

[88] Dulux. *Dulux Weathershield Gloss Datasheet.* URL http://www.duspec.com.au/duspec/file/AUDD0054.pdf. Date accessed. June 16, 2015.

[89] Wattyl. *Wattyl Solagard Ultra Premium Low Sheen. Data Sheet*. URL http://www.wattyl.com.au/export/download/product_datasheet/D4.14_-_Solagard_Low_Sheen.pdf?pdf. Date accessed. July 16, 2015.

[90] Taubmans. *Sunproof.* URL. http://www.taubmans.com.au/Paints/Sun-Proof. Date accessed. June 16, 2015.

[91] The instructions on the Accents SolarMax can. Date viewed July 17, 2015

[92] Timber Queensland *Technical Datasheet 5, Cypress and Hardwood Cladding*. (Brisbane: Self Published, 2014), 1. Bootle is less definitive with the term "often used". *Wood ...*, 151.

[93] Timber Queensland. *Technical Datasheet 2, Finishes for Exterior Timber*. (Brisbane: Self Published, 2014), 1.

performance of the premium acrylics. There can be no substitute for obtaining a written recommendation for a primer and top coat from reputable suppliers especially when new formulations are being released.

Pine poses extra problems as it would be expected that there will be some untreated, low durability, heartwood in the mix. Up to 20% of the cross section is allowed to be untreated but can be much higher due to some poor quality material selection and treatment that is occurring. Water based primers are normally water permeable and can trap moisture under the paint and promote decay.

A successful[94] painted furniture project will include the following:

- A light colour will be chosen to extend the life of the paint and timber[95]
- There will be no housed joints
- The ends will be sealed
- The primer will be checked for adhesion if factory applied, and
- The top coat will be applied by brush.

Clear Film finishes

More care needs to be taken when considering whether to use a clear finish on external furniture than with penetrating oil. These films can easily be the "maintenance nightmare" that has been referred to earlier. Many professionals have reported very disappointing results to me and a reluctance, even an outright refusal, to use them. This poor performance is something I have also observed in many projects and experienced firsthand. Film finishes have to deal with the same variability mentioned under the *Paint* section above which cause many of the problems but not all.

Figure 75. Project finished with clear film finish.

UV blockers are a critical component of clear film finishes. The finish should contain blockers that protect the timber and different blockers that protect the film itself. These blockers are expensive and some low priced finishes have neither! Without the blockers that protect the timber, the fibres start to break down into a fine powder, indiscernible to the naked eye. Once this happens you have a member that is, in effect, wrapped in cling film. The microclimate between the wood and the film can then hasten decay. Any break in the film, which can be caused by natural feature (Refer Figure 77), unsealed butt joints, or fasteners can also allow moisture to enter and promote decay. As mentioned under the Leaching section above, the extractives found in

---

[94] One of my proof readers asked me to share his experience of problems associated with painting with the hope that closer attention will be given to painting specifications generally. He had specified LVL rafters which extended past the house which were coated with a waterbased paint. The rafters were to have a polycarbonate roof over them protecting them from the elements. Unknown to him the client deleted this covering as funds were short and as a consequence the LVL's "wet rotted" under the paint. The paint manufacturer replied that some water based paints were "pervious" i.e. that they let water through to the timber and trapping it and not letting the water escape.

[95] Dark colours can make the timber overheat increased checking can result which allows the ingress of moisture.

hardwood can cause the film to break down from the inside out which is why most clear finish manufacturers recommend a leaching period of something like six to eight weeks. But remember, in our drought prone land, if it has not rained, which it might well not have done over an eight week period, it has not leached so you may have to introduce washing, or better still chemical pre-leaching as part of the coating plan. Do not expect recycled timber to be pre-leached. The finish should also be of a thick consistency so forcing the painter to put on a heavy coat.[96]

Figure 76.   CN oil on deck and clear film on battens.

Figure 77.   Decay in spotted gum under a premium film finish after eighteen months.

Figure 78.   Film finish on battens.[97]

Figure 79.   Film breaking down.

The Achilles heel of film finishes is maintenance. If the film is left to deteriorate it will need to be completely sanded back to bare timber between coats. This means that frequently, if not usually, recoating simply isn't done. If it is recoated, and it will need to be done on a very regular basis, it will be a costly exercise as the timber should be sanded between coats though, if frequent enough, the painter may not have to sand back to bare timber prior to recoating. The cost of this maintenance should be discussed with the client at design stage. Film finishes are suitable for internal furniture however.

---

[96] I am aware of one project in North Queensland where the painter applied three thin coats and after an expensive claim the manufacturer reformulated the finish.

[97] This fence is a good example of the use of sawmill recovery sizes.

These finishes can be used over rough sawn timber but it is necessary to sand before the first coat otherwise a very rough finish results. Manufacturer's recommendations on dressed timber can include a further sand between subsequent coats. Under no circumstances use steel wool to sand as rust marks can develop on the timber.

Penetrating Oils

There is little doubt that the most robust penetrating oil that can be applied is CN oil (refer the decking in Figure 76 which is coated in CN Oil).[98] The abbreviation CN stands for copper napthenate and the oil is a registered preservative. Against this superior performance is the unavoidable fact that, when it is first applied, it looks horrendous and the smell is not very inviting either. On top it takes a long time to not rub off on clothing.[99] This means that any oil chosen will not be the best available for the timber but a compromise between serviceability and functionality.

As for any oil other than CN, none will work as a preservative. To make that claim the product must be registered with the APVMA and, at the time of writing, none are.[100] If you have not received the correct natural durability nor treated the sapwood correctly you cannot make everything well by using an oil, even an expensive one. The main things you can expect from a penetrating oil is that it works as a water repellant and a UV blocker. The same thing can be said about UV blockers in oils as with clear

Figure 80.   Freshly applied penetrating oil. **Architect:** Ralph Bailey. **Material**: Iron bark.

finishes. They are expensive and some products can have very little of them. Indeed they can have very little water repellency as well. Fortunately, unlike paint and clear films, penetrating oils are not affected by dimensional change.[101]

---

[98] CN oil (or similar and I do not know of a similar) is the product recommended for architectural battens by Colin Mackenzie, Technical Consultant, Timber Queensland. *Pers. Com.* April 24, 2015.

[99] It was this inability to reapply in waterways that prompted us to work with Lonza to develop Tanacoat. Some oils at the time contained some very unsuitable additives for use over water.

[100] I was responsible for having one brand which was making this claim reported to the APVMA. If you hear anyone making this claim you need to check it with the APVMA.

[101] Bootle. *Wood...*, 146.

Figure 81.   Un-oiled spotted gum

Figure 82.   Same piece of spotted gum oiled with Tanacoat light oak[102]

Unfortunately, the UV blockers will darken the timber somewhat as can be seen in Figure 81 and Figure 82 where Tanacoat, a decking oil with a significant amount of oil, has been applied, The before and after views are on the same piece of spotted gum. The addition of tints will increase the longevity of any penetrating oil. The author encountered a situation where any change in colour of a light coloured hardwood due to the UV blockers was unacceptable to the client. In this case the customer agreed to the use of seven coats of a premium brand oil without UV blockers[103] and then three monthly re-applications. This level of maintenance is outside of what would normally be accepted.

People confuse penetrating oil with film finish as, when the oils are first applied, it does have some level of gloss finish but this is frequently short-lived, especially on unseasoned timber. That does not mean it is not present and not working. Pour water on the surface and you could well find that it is still repelling water. Once the surface stops repelling moisture it is time to reapply. Unlike film finishes there is no need to sand back at all, simply wash off any dust and kill any mould if present[104] and then re-\apply. This simplicity and relatively low cost makes maintenance far more likely.

How can you tell a good penetrating oil from one that is less so? Glossy cans and brochures and a high price are not necessarily a reliable guide and marketing claims should not be accepted on face value. Technical data sheets also don't necessarily show the relevant information required to determine a "good quality" product. The saying "oils ain't oils" stands true. A good quality oil should contain ingredients like:

- Resin system or oil suitable for timber. Often resins are modified to have characteristics which address limitations of natural oils. This can include mould growth in linseed oil and lanolin
- UV absorbers which offer protection to timber substrate and resin/oil system
- Water repellents. These can vary significantly in type and quality and should not be prone to mould e.g. again linseed oil and lanolin
- Mould and algae inhibitors (These will not remove or prevent mould from pre-infected timber.) and
- Solvent carrier that aids in penetration of ingredients into timber.

---

[102] Light Oak is untinted Tanacoat. The colour change is due to the UV blockers.
[103] The product chosen was Sikkens Sadolin Hardwood Oil. It may have required a monthly reapplication during summer.
[104] This requires more than bleach, an active biocide is also required as in products similar to Exit Mould.

On this last point there are many types of solvent systems. Many penetrating oil formulations contain petroleum based solvents of varying flash points and levels of aromatics as well as those which have surfactants to allow water to be incorporated. The best penetrating oils contain a petroleum based solvent system as it is more able to penetrate the timber and less prone to facilitate movement of tannins to the surface. A product which incorporates a solvent with a high flashpoint and low aromatics would be preferable. What does this mean? A high flashpoint (above 60.5 degrees C) will mean the product will not be considered flammable thus reducing risks for transport, storage and use. A low aromatic solvent will reduce odour and risk often associated with using solvents. While these features do not necessarily add to the quality of a product they do provide benefits which make oil based penetrating oils more amenable to use and hence get the best result in timber.[105]

Figure 83. Oiled hardwood decking with a black discoloration.

If you are going to maintain your external furniture by applying multiple coats over time, those oils containing copper should be avoided as this will tend to blacken the timber. Oils containing linseed oil should also be rejected as mold can grow on the timber and the rags can spontaneously combust. This may be referred to as "seed oil" in the MSDS. The timber in Figure 83 is an Australian hardwood but its natural beauty has been lost through a black discoloration which is typical of either the presence of copper and the use of linseed oil.

Lanolin Based Oils

Lanolin based products are sometimes chosen as they are perceived as being the environmentally friendly answer but, with the wool grease content possibly as low as 10%, and the petroleum based solvents at more than 60%, it is arguable if this is, in fact, the case.[106] It is probably no better or no worse than any other oil in this regard. This is a totally different issue to whether this particular finish works well or not. Again, we can find unsubstantiated claims of preservation from this type of product.[107] There is a long way from protecting the floors of shearing sheds under a roof to giving the same performance in fully weather exposed applications. Mould growth can be an issue and inhibitors are required to address it.

---

[105] All of these points were considered in the development of Tanacoat. When you are considering specifying a penetrating oil you need to ask probing questions of the manufacturer to ensure you are asking for a product that is at least equal.

[106] Lanoteck. *Lanotec Timber Seal Material Safety Data Sheet*. URL: http://lanotec.liveserver.com.au/wp-content/uploads/2014/04/MSDS-Timber-Seal.pdf. Date accessed. June 22, 2015.

[107] Deck Doc..*About Deck Doc* URL: http://www.deckdoc.com.au/about Date accessed. October 29, 2017. I easily found four other references to Lanolin being a preservative or reducing wood rot. My understanding at the time of writing is that no lanolin producer has had these claims verified.

Painting Steel Frames

The recommendations for painting steel frames is covered in the chapter on frames.

9 Applying Finishes and Maintenance

The previous chapter spoke generally about timber finishes and once a finish type has been chosen, if indeed any finish is chosen, it is necessary to be very specific about how the product is going to be applied. Instructions do vary between manufacturers e.g. whether leaching is required before applying oils and, if so, how much weathering is needed. Also, site specific recommendations such as the number of coats can change if the exposure is considered extreme. The frequency and method of maintenance also needs to be nominated. I would class all weather exposed applications in Australia as extreme.

Oil Based Finishes

As mentioned, the recommendations for applying different penetrating oils vary between manufacturers. The recommendations provided to me from one leading manufacturer, Sikkens, for refined architectural pieces is as follows. A similar approach would be used with the product I normally use, Tanacoat.

Consideration with new or recycled timber

If starting with new or recycled hardwood

- Begin by cleaning and removing tannins, oils and extractives using Cetol BL Tannin and Oil Remover followed by Cetol BL Deck and Woodcleaner
- After cleaning the surfaces need to be allowed to dry for a minimum of three to four good drying days to ensure any moisture trapped in joins, gaps, cracks, screw and nail holes time to dry thoroughly
- Ensure all square/sharp edges are rounded over
- Sand only if raising of the grain is evident. No finer than 180 grit recommended
- Dust off and apply a minimum of four coats of Cetol HLSe[108] by brush (Natural bristle preferably) or a coarse grade synthetic to ensure a good protective film thickness. (No Spraying, rollers, applicators or pads). Four coats are recommended in an extreme UV area
- if there is a noticeable raising of the grain after the first coat, sand lightly with 180 grit abrasive only. Sanding is not recommended between subsequent coats
- Allow a minimum of 24 hours drying between coats ensuring each coat is properly dry before applying subsequent coats. After the final coat is applied allow five to seven days to fully cure before subjecting furniture to normal usage

Maintenance when penetrating oil finish is in good condition

Maintenance should be carried out whenever there is a noticeable diminishing of sheen level. In an extreme UV area we would suggest a six monthly inspection with a maintenance coat applied as required. If passing the six monthly inspection, the asset owner may choose to inspect monthly thereafter. As the coating cannot be expected to last 12 months it is probably best simply to recoat every six months. The process is:

---

[108] Cetol HLSe a highly transparent exterior finish available in a number of transparent shades. The darker the colour / pigment the greater UV protection from the sun.

- Wash surfaces with a mild detergent and water to remove dirt, grease, oil, salt etc
- Allow surfaces to dry thoroughly
- Sand lightly using 180 grit minimum abrasive to etch new coating to old
- Reapply sufficient coats of Cetol HLSe to re-establish suggested minimum four coat coating thickness

Maintenance with oil when film finish has started to deteriorate

- All previous coatings need to be removed i.e. sanded back to bare wood. 80 - 120 grit abrasive recommended.
- Treat any areas where mould is evident with a mixture of Pure Oil of Cloves and Water. Mixing a 1/4 teaspoon of Oil of Cloves to 1litre of clean water will generally kill mould spores and inhibit regrowth. Oil of Cloves is better than bleach as bleach doesn't kill the spores but merely bleaches them and they will regrow.
- After cleaning, surfaces need to be allowed to dry for a minimum of three to four good drying days to ensure any moisture trapped in joins, gaps, cracks, screw and nail holes time to dry thoroughly.
- Ensure all square/sharp edges are rounded over.
- Sand only if raising of the grain is evident. No finer than 180 grit recommended.
- Dust off and apply a minimum of four coats of Cetol HLSe[109] by brush (Natural bristle preferably) or a coarse grade synthetic to ensure a good protective film thickness. (No Spraying, rollers, applicators or pads). Four coats are recommended in an extreme UV area
- Sand lightly after first coat with 180 grit abrasive only if there is a noticeable raising of the grain. Sanding is not recommended between subsequent coats.
- Allow a minimum of 24 hours drying between coats ensuring each coat is properly dry before applying subsequent coats. After the final coat is applied allow 5 to 7 days to fully cure before subjecting furniture to normal usage.

Marine Varnish Finish

The following specification was supplied by Goran Stevanovic[110] on using Feast Watson Weatherproof Polyurethane Varnish. Goran has experience with this material when used in high profile venues relatively close to the water's edge. He advised that as long as the finish is maintained to a high standard, it will normally perform satisfactorily but is aware that few owners will commit to these costs. He also advised that in a venue with salt spray and cooling misters in place, this type of finish was not a success.[111] This reinforces the wisdom of a written manufacturers recommendation and even wiser, use an oil finish.

---

[109] Cetol HLSe is a highly transparent exterior woodstain available in a number of transparent shades. The darker the colour/pigment the greater UV protection from the sun.

[110] At the time of writing, Goran was a project manager with Redwood Carpentry, Matraville, NSW.

[111] Factors that can impact on the life of this type of finish is simply the number of "bums on seats" causing wear and the associated sweat and body oils combined with salt spray that have been observed to be corrosive to film finishes. Koch. Steven. *Pers. Com.* 2 May 2018.

- Sand back to bare timber, finishing with 180 grit and fill all cracks and imperfections with a clear epoxy filler, refilling till an even smooth surface is achieved. The epoxy must be compatible with the Feast Watson
- Dust off and apply four coats of Feast Watson Weatherproof Varnish, allowing 12 hours drying between coats, applying the final coat within 30 hours of the previous coat.
- Monitor condition closely, inspecting tables every two weeks initially to identify any new splits or damage. As soon as a split or damage occurs remove the table from service and refinish as follows. Clean the surface with a compatible cleaner to remove any grease or surface contaminants, sand lightly, refill splits with a clear polyurethane epoxy filler, and repaint, applying 2 primer coats locally and 2 coats overall as above.
- Experience suggests that the first service coat may be required within 3 months. However as the timber stabilises in its exposure, refinishing will be required less often. Eventually, requiring refinishing every 6 to 8 months.
- After finishing, allow to cure for 3 days prior to putting the table back into service.

These recommendations, both for oil and varnish, are "off label" but one was supplied by the finish manufacturer and another by an experienced fabricator. They demonstrate how the locality can affect the specification on a job by job basis. As mentioned, I strongly advise that after you chose your finish style and brand that you obtain a written site specific specification for its application and maintenance and ask about any warranty.

10 Thinking Away From the Standards

As was mentioned in the discussion on Australian Standards, there are many furniture items that are not addressed, such as backless chairs and platforms. This series of images show useful furniture items that, for one reason or other, do not comply with our Standards but most are innovative and useful additions to the space they are in.

In Figure 84 a fairly standard barbecue table at the University of Queensland, St Lucia campus has a very unusual seating arrangement. Students can recline and the triangular setting allows strangers to share the one setting without invading each other's privacy by sitting back to back.

Figure 84.   Unusual seating arrangement at University of Queensland, St Lucia.

Often people want to do more than sit in a public space. The unit in Figure 85, part of my own product line-up allows the user to sit, recline or semi recline. The flat surfaces accommodate books, food and drinks.

Figure 85.   Multi use setting built by the author.

The platforms in Figure 86 situated in Gatton, Queensland were supplied by the author and again were part of my standard product range. They were very popular with the café patrons.

Figure 86.   A series of platforms

Figure 87.   Seating, Budapest, Hungary.

The author supplied the seats shown in Figure 87 in Budapest, Hungary. The unusual shape was driven by the understanding that strangers do not like to sit next to each other so personal space was provided.

The backless unit in Figure 88 built on a stainless frame with sawmill recovery size timber can double as a "day bed". It also is an acknowledgement that people want to do more than sit in a public area.

Figure 88.   Day bed, Cairns Esplanade

A four sided seat in Figure 89 situated in Nantwich, England has been built around a planter box. The unit gives life to a large open space. It would not meet back height and angle requirements of the Australian Standard but does have an armrest.

Figure 89.   Planter box, Nantwich, England..

The very simple and effective seat in Figure 90 situated in a park in Cheltenham, England was achieved by using just three pieces of timber.

Figure 90.   Simple seat, Cheltenham UK..

The seating near the waterfront in Auckland, New Zealand is extremely flexible. The units are on rollers so they can be situated to suit the size of the groups and adjust personal space to the users' needs. They are large enough to use as beds but also have adjustable backrests that can which allow people to semi recline.

Figure 91.   Adjustable settings in Auckland, New Zealand.

The curved backless seat of Figure 92 at the Melbourne Botanical Gardens is made unusually attractive by the use of irregularly shaped timber elements.

Figure 92.   Curved seating at Melbourne Botanical Gardens.

Figure 93.   Seating at Institute for Lifelong Learning, Izumigo, Japan.

The seats in Figure 93 are situated at the Institute of Lifelong Learning at the resort area of Izumigo, Japan. Without back or arm rests these seats would not comply with Australian Standards. But this image highlights the architects attempt to fully integrate the furniture with the landscaping. This project was supplied by the author.

The seating unit/platform in Auckland is sized so that it can be more than just seating. It is made up of ex 100x100 timbers which is much heavier than is found in most timber furniture.

Figure 94.   Platform in Auckland, New Zealand uses larger size timber elements.

11 Design Checklist

Project Name	
My application is	
Internal	
External under roof	
Fully external	
Possibly all of the above	
My timber choice	
Pine	
I have addressed the possibility of poor performance of pine external furniture by:	
Cypress	
I have addressed the possibility of poor performance of cypress external furniture to dry out excessively and crack by:	
Australian hardwood	
I have addressed the possibility of receiving lower performing Australian hardwood external furniture by:	
Other hardwood - imported	
I have addressed the possibility of poor performance by some imported hardwood external furniture by:	
Note: Ensure the supplier is referring to Australian durability standards.	
Timber Grade	
I have included a specification for the species I have chosen.	Yes　　No
I have used a different specification to the one suggested in the *External Timber Furniture* guide for the species chosen because:	
Kiln Drying	
The timber is kiln dried?	Yes　　No
I have considered the need for kiln dried timber and my reasons for my decision are:	
Note: Timber above 50 mm cannot be dried commercially and requesting KD timber when	

not required could add 3 months to delivery of the timber.			
Timber Treatment Note: Supply of untreated sapwood in any timber is not an option.			
Pine: I have countered the possibility of receiving poorly treated pine by: Tip: For waterborne preservatives look at the dark coloration at the end – must be at least 80% of cross section I have ensured that I do not receive CCA treated pine by:			
Cypress: Because it resists waterborne preservatives I have specified LOSP and have researched a treatment plant that can treat it to refusal, not absorption. That plant is: Note: Cypress will have to be kiln dried and so not larger than 50 mm			
Hardwood: I have specified the sapwood to be treated to H3 Tip: LOSP can be used only on KD timber and treatment is done on green off saw timber to prevent insect attack during drying so preservatives must be waterborne. I have ensured that I do not receive CCA treated hardwood by:			
Imported Hardwood: I have spoken to my supplier about the presence of sapwood and he advised: Note: Obtain a written recommendation.			
Overordering of Timber			
My specification requires the supplier to overorder the timber	Yes		No
I require the timber be overorder by what percentage Tip: Depending on difficulty of receiving replacements this should start at 5%			
Timber Sizes			
I have confirmed that the sizes required can be supplied Tip: Remember nominal size is reduced by sawing tolerance, kiln drying and machining			
Do I require evidence that timber has been ordered in time	Yes		No
Recycled Timber			
I am aware that recycled timber re-sawn from larger sizes will be unseasoned. This affects my specification how?			
I am aware that industry grades for recycled timber are very low. This affects my specification how?			

Sawmill Recovery Sizes		
I have given consideration to the use of sawmill recovery sizes ex 50x25 through to 75x38?	Yes	No
If "Yes" I have identified and mentioned a supplier and lead time? That is:		
Glued Timber		
I have permitted glued joints?	Yes	No
If "Yes" I am going to make this succeed by: Warning: This is highly unlikely to succeed.		
Round Timber		
I have included round timber in my design?	Yes	No
If "Yes" I have considered how to achieve the size I require without gluing. How will this be achieved? Note: Approx. 42 mm is the maximum that can be achieved from KD solid timber.		
Detailing Frames and Fasteners		
The furniture uses frames not made of timber?	Yes	No
The frames are made of standard section steel?	Yes	No
I have checked the availability of the sizes specified?	Yes	No
The steel is to be galvanised after fabrication?	Yes	No
If galvanised, what thickness coating is required?		
I have excluded lightly galvanised products such as "Duragal"?	Yes	No
The frames are made of laser cut steel?	Yes	No
If laser cut, I have checked the availability of the plate needed?	Yes	No
If laser cut, I have allowed sufficient grip if folding is required?	Yes	No
The frames are made from stainless steel?	Yes	No
If stainless, have specified the grade?	Yes	No
The grade is?		
If stainless, I have checked the polish required?	Yes	No
The polish is?		
I have checked that the fasteners are available?	Yes	No
Given that there is now no Australian Standard for screws, how have I ensured appropriate screws will be used?		
The frames will be painted?	Yes	No
Is the paint finish also the anti-corrosion protection?	Yes	No
I have a written specification for painting the steel?	Yes	No
This is reflected in the specification?	Yes	No
Timber Detailing – Standard Sizes		
I am face fixing the timber slats to timber?	Yes	No

How am I avoiding splitting any timber support by having screws in a straight line along the grain?		
Have I included housed joints that may decay prematurely?	Yes	No
Does the table have a perimeter trim?	Yes	No
Have I avoided slope of grain issues associated with round tables?	Yes	No
Have I given thought to achieving a safe trouble-free corner?	Yes	No
Do I have large unsupported overhangs and spans between the legs	Yes	No
Timber Detailing – Large Sizes		
Does my design contain large section sizes?	Yes	No
Are sizes with a cross section less than 175 mm specified heart free? E.g. sizes such as 150x150, 200x150,	Yes	No
How have I ensured there will be no substitution with heart in timber? Note: This material is difficult to supply and substitution is frequent		
Have I detailed expansion joints in sizes 200 mm and over?	Yes	No
Have I protected vertical heart with a cap?	Yes	No
Have very large sizes been detailed with effective anti-split plates?	Yes	No
Has a time limit been imposed for installing these plates?	Yes	No
Leaching and Finishing		
Is this a project where pre-leaching is required?	Yes	No
If "Yes" how will this be done? Note: pine and cypress will not need pre-leaching.		
Will the furniture will be pre-finished?	Yes	No
Finishing with Paint		
Am I aware that a poor paint choice can promote decay?	Yes	No
I have a written specification from the manufacturer for the location?	Yes	No
Finishing with Clear Film Finish		
Am I aware that many professionals report very poor results?	Yes	No
Has the high maintenance costs been discussed with client?	Yes	No
Do I have a written spec from the manufacturer for the location?	Yes	No
I have a written advice from the manufacturer for maintenance?	Yes	No
Is there a record of this being supplied to the customer?	Yes	No
Finishing with Penetrating Oils		
I have excluded oils containing linseed oil and/or copper?	Yes	No
Do I have a written spec from the manufacturer for the location?	Yes	No
Has maintenance been discussed with the client?	Yes	No
I have written advice from the manufacturer on maintenance?	Yes	No
Is there a record of this being supplied to the customer?	Yes	No
I have asked for APVMA recognition of claims to be a preservative?	Yes	No
Checklist Completed By		
Date		

Source of Images

Images not listed below are part of the author's collection.

Figure	Image	Copyright holder
Figure 1	Eames chair	Sourced from Wikipedia
Figure 4	Fabricated frame	Dennis Clark Photography
Figure 10	Triangular table	Dennis Clark Photography
Figure 12	Pine failure	John Huth
Figure 21	200x200 splitting	Dennis Clark Photography
Figure 24	Twisted boards	Ralph Bailey
Figure 30	Jimmy Possum chair	Jeff Keyes
Figure 31	Log seats	Evangeline Graham
Figure 52	Round table	Gary Hopewell
0	Posts separated from ground	James Stubbersfield
Figure 67	NSW barbecue table	Dennis Clark Photography
Figure 71	Stone building	Panekyo, Japan
Figure 72	Sap stain	Steve Mitchell
Figure 73	Leaching sap	Nigel Shaw
Figure 74	Decay under clear finish	Martin Perkowicz
Figure 77	Decay under film finish	Nigel Shaw
Figure 83	Discolouration under finish	Ralph Bailey
Figure 84	Uni Queensland seating	Gary Hopewell
Figure 91	Adjustable seating, Auckland	Evan Blackledge
Figure 92	Curved seating, Melbourne	Shutterstock
Figure 94	Platform, Auckland	Evan Blackledge

Bibliography

Bootle, Keith R. *Wood in Australia, Types Properties and Uses, Second Edition.* (Sydney; McGraw Hill, 1983).

Hyne *Technical Data Sheet 6*, (No publication data, May 14).

Landmark. *Maintenance Guide Document SLF 002-2.* (Deception Bay: Landmark Products, UD).

Queensland Government. *Queensland Parks and Wildlife Services Manual May 2003.* (No publication details)

Standards Australia. *AS1428.2 – 1992 Design for access and mobility – Enhanced and additional requirements – Buildings and facilities.* (Homebush: Standards Australia, 1997).

Standards Australia. *AS2082-2000 Timber—Hardwood—Visually stressgraded for structural purposes* (Strathfield: Standards Australia International Ltd, 2000).

Standards Australia. *AS2796.1-1999 Timber—Hardwood—Sawn and milled products Part 1: Product specification* (Strathfield: Standards Australia International Ltd, 1999).

Standards Australia. *AS5604-2003 Timber—Natural durability ratings.* (Sydney: Standards Australia International Ltd, 2003).

Standards Australia. *AS4785.2-2002 Timber - Softwood - Sawn and milled products Grade description* (Sydney: Standards Australia International Ltd, 2002).

Stirling, Rod. *Natural Durability Classification Systems Used Around the World.* Paper presented at The International Research Group On Wood Protection conference, Beijing, China May 2009. Reference: IRG/WP 09-10694.

Timber Queensland. *Technical Datasheet 2, Finishes for Exterior Timber.* (Brisbane: Timber Queensland, 2014).

Timber Queensland *Technical Datasheet 5, Cypress and Hardwood Cladding.* (Brisbane: Timber Queensland, 2014).

Internet Sites

Auswest Timbers. *Karri Hardwood Furniture.* URL: http://auswesttimbers.com.au/product/karri-hardwood-furniture/ Date accessed: 7 October 2017.

Botton and Gardiner. *Environmental Policy.* URL: http://www.bottonandgardiner.com.au/about-us/environmental-policy Date Accessed: October 4, 2017.

Deck Doc. *About Deck Doc* URL: http://www.deckdoc.com.au/about Date accessed: October 29, 2017.

Department of Agriculture and Fisheries. *Jarrah*. URL: https://www.daf.qld.gov.au/forestry/using-wood-and-its-benefits/wood-properties-of-timber-trees/jarrah. Date Accessed: 3 October 2017.

Department of Agriculture and Fisheries. *Spotted Gum*. URL: https://www.daf.qld.gov.au/forestry/using-wood-and-its-benefits/wood-properties-of-timber-trees/spotted-gum. Date Accessed: 3 October 2017.

Department of Agriculture and Fisheries. *Tallowwood*. URL: https://www.daf.qld.gov.au/forestry/using-wood-and-its-benefits/wood-properties-of-timber-trees/tallowwood. Date Accessed: 3 October 2017.

Department of Agriculture and Fisheries. *Tasmanian Oak*. URL: https://www.daf.qld.gov.au/forestry/using-wood-and-its-benefits/wood-properties-of-timber-trees/tasmanian-oak. Date Accessed: 3 October 2017.

Department of Agriculture and Fisheries. *White Cypress*. URL: https://www.daf.qld.gov.au/forestry/using-wood-and-its-benefits/wood-properties-of-timber-trees/white-cypress. Date Accessed: 3 October 2017.

Intergrain. *Dimension 4 Ultra Primer*. URL: http://www.intergrain.com.au/product-selector/product-detail/intergrain-ultraprimer. Date accessed. 29 October 2017.

Lanoteck. *Lanotec Timber Seal Material Safety Data Sheet*. URL: http://lanotec.liveserver.com.au/wp-content/uploads/2014/04/MSDS-Timber-Seal.pdf. Date accessed. June 22, 2015.

Norton, Jack *Managing Timber Durability*. URL: http://www.timberqueensland.com.au/Docs/News%20and%20Events/Events/Jack-Norton_treatment.pdf. Date accessed: 27 April 2018.

Parkside timbers. *Parkside Structural and Joinery Products* URL: http://parksidetimber.com.au/structural-joinery.html. Date accessed:9 October 2017.

Tietz, Christian. *People-friendly furniture in public places matters more than ever in today's city* URL: https://theconversation.com/people-friendly-furniture-in-public-places-matters-more-than-ever-in-todays-city-83568 Date Accessed: June 8, 2018.

TTT Products. *Multipole*. URL: http://www.unilog.co.nz/product-31-ttt-multipoles--foundations. Date Accessed: October 2, 2017.

About the Author

I have over 40 years' experience the timber industry, having managed timber processing and manufacturing businesses. I am now a Senior Timber Consultant providing my expertise to both the private and government sectors. My previous company, Outdoor Structures Australia (OSA), became recognised as Australia's foremost authority on weather exposed timber structures. OSA manufactured and supplied decking, boardwalks, bridges and landscaping to many government departments and developers. I am also Australia's leading author on timber related subjects, having published 19 guides, and am in demand as a presenter and trainer.